T0128017

DIVINE GODHEAD
WITH
DIVINE PRINCIPLE
AND
PATTERN

L.O. LAWAL

WESTBOW
PRESS®
A DIVISION OF THOMAS NELSON
& ZONDERVAN

WestBow Press books may be ordered through booksellers or by contacting:

WestBow Press
A Division of Thomas Nelson & Zondervan
1663 Liberty Drive
Bloomington, IN 47403
www.westbowpress.com
1 (866) 928-1240

ISBN: 978-1-5127-5537-4 (sc)
ISBN: 978-1-5127-5538-1 (hc)
ISBN: 978-1-5127-5536-7 (e)

Library of Congress Control Number: 2016914345

Print information available on the last page.

WestBow Press rev. date: 9/14/2016

CONTENTS

ACKNOWLEDGMENT

I wholeheartedly acknowledged the Divine Godhead for their massive grace upon my life for almost forty years of my journey on earth.

I also remain eternally grateful to divine Godhead for my beautiful Hearts of God families, friends and associates He has given me in life. You know, we all have two families on Earth; we got the one we are born with and the one God in His infinite mercy one way or the other brought on our way to choose as we sojourn here on Earth to heaven and I am gladly declare to choose you all.

The making of this book was by a divine foreknowing and the process of divine revelations through the Spirit which came as a confirmation by these two wonderful members of Family of God.

In the year 2000, Brother Adewale J. Aderogba asked me if I could write a book and in 2009, Deaconess Vivian Oghenejobo mentioned it that I should write a book this is the same word of encouragements.

In 2011, it was strongly placed in my heart to gathered and pen down all that the Lord Almighty had done for me, still doing through me and in confirmation to His Divine WORD both in Rhema (Spoken) and Logos (Written).

This is a book written with my proven personal Testimonies in each topic discussed; that I am sure will be an helping tools in the hands of young ones growing up to meet the divine standard of God and to those that are truly seeking the mind and the Existence of the divine Godhead; and I have trust that there will be Spiritual and all round blessings as a results of this book.

The book will also help in appreciating the Divine Godhead more in our Lives.

I THANK YOU ALL

OVERVIEW

For all believers, it is important to hear what the Word of God says on any matter or issues; of no less importance is the subject on the Principles and Patterns of the Sovereign God on Earth. This is something that has perhaps a tremendous effect on a person's life and eternity.

When Christians are seeking a solution to any part of their life or any matter that affect their entire life and that of their environment, it is essential for them to seek the mind and will of God. There should be an enquiry, because God Almighty, the Creator of Heaven and Earth alone have the general plans and blueprints of His divine projects on His hand, and also for an individual on earth.

The Scripture made it clear in 1Chronicle 13:7-14, I will like you to read this passage carefully, especially verses 9-11. Here, you discovered that something was missing somewhere, as the Principles and Patterns of God were not followed; that is what happen when we think we can help God with our human doctrine, philosophy, and ideals that are not solely based on the Scriptures; as we are not immediately or always aware of the dangers that follow and more also affect the innocent and our Loved one.

According to the verses read above, we might think this was Uzza's fault for touching the Ark of God, but really, it was king David's fault, because he had Uzza and Ahio to put the Ark in a cart, when it was supposed to be carried on poles, only by the Levites (the priest tribe) and on their Shoulders Exodus 25:10-15 and Numbers 4:15-20.

Therefore, had he followed the Lord's clear directions for moving the ark, it would never have stumbled, and Uzzah would never have reached out to steady it? Also, a Levite would have known not to touch the ark, because he would have been trained on how to handle the Ark of God - but Uzzah was not a chosen Levite, he was a normal man, and never should have been carrying it, so in his ignorance, he reached out to steady it, and was struck dead. This is an example of God chastening David, reminding him that there is a right and wrong way to serve him, and he should not let his good intentions get confused for God's will. So, the challenge for us here is to not let our good ideas or good intentions get confused with God's will just because they sound good to us, and the people who are our counsellors seem to agree with us. We need to return to the Lord and see if any cause of actions; is His will or not, and also; seek Him about how to carry His Assignments out, this is very compulsory. How often do we do things out of our own strength and our own understanding, not really seeking the Lord? How often do I get a good idea, and just run with it instead of seeking God through Prayer and in His Divine Word?

The principle and Patterns of God remain unchanged; Psalm119:152, either we believe this or we forget it, one thing I am sure of, is that; the commandment and the will of Godhead are not burdensome rather they are of great blessings and Eternal unto us. Matthew 11:28-29. Whenever, we do the right thing the way God ordained them, that which was a death we definitely turn to great blessing 1 Chronicle 15:11-16, Exodus 39:42-43, 40:33-38 2 Chronicle 7:1.

How many times in life even up till now people are following the way of Uzzah and forget about the Principles and Patterns of God – He who is the owner of all His divine Projects on Earth. We decides for God how to run His Project and He decided to sometimes play along with us and we think that He is happy and blesses our foolishness, disobedience, and pride. No; I mean Capital NO - there is no way God will tick right His permissive will above His perfect will. 2 Peter 3:9, 15, Ezekiel 33:11, 1 Timothy 2:3-4, Roman 6:1, 15

God said in His Word 'The Way of Life and Death have I shown you; but, I beseech you, choose Life' The Blessed God did not make us a robot; He expect us to be like the Bereans, compare our activities in Life with the scriptures and make used of our common senses by applying whatever we hear, see and feel inside is Eternal Manual 'The Bible'. Act 17:10-12.

It is most interesting that more space is devoted to the account of the Tabernacle in the Scriptures than any other single object. In the book of Exodus chapters 25-40, it gives details of the plans and construction of the Tabernacle or Tent of Meeting. Moreover, the New Testament makes figurative reference to the Tabernacle and its furnishings, and the Epistle to the Hebrews cannot be understood without knowledge of the books of Exodus and Leviticus and the book of Hebrews is the best commentary on them.

In the Old Testament and History of Tabernacle, we find that God dwells among His chosen people.

"Let them construct a sanctuary for me (God) that I may dwell among them. According to all that I am going to show you, as the pattern of the tabernacle and the pattern of all its furniture, "just so you shall construct it" (Exodus 25:8-9), Exodus 27:21. The Tabernacle symbolized the dwelling place of God in the midst of His people.

"There I will meet with you; and from above the mercy seat, from between the two cherubim which are upon the ark of the testimony, I will speak to you about all that I will give you in commandment for the sons of Israel" (v. 22). "The Tabernacle was a symbol of God's dwelling.

There is a Sanctuary, wherein is the special residence and manifestation of the glorious presence of God … Almost all expressions which are employed in describing the significance of the Tabernacle are also used in reference to Heaven." Ezekiel 43:10-12, 44:5.

There is a need for us as the Pilgrims of Heaven that before accepting any doctrine or precepts, we should demand a plain 'Thus says the Lord' Either in Rhema the spoken word from the Mouth of God or Logos the written Word of His Eternal Holy Book 'The Bible' 'Yet; the two must cordially agree; anything outside this, is not God Jeremiah 23:28-29. Ezekiel 13:3, 1 Corinthians 3:12-13, in other words, we need to remember that our Feelings and thoughts have to be scrutinized and be in tune with divine Spirit of God before taking any course of actions 1Thessalonians 5:21.

Are you willing to commit yourself to those Principles and Patterns both in purpose for your living on earth, in ministry, spiritually, in Marriage and in all your relationships and Endeavour? There can be no better counsel than what is found in the Word of God and this is where the right guidelines for our directions can be found and also, believe me; this is the Major and Primary step in fulfilling your destiny with God's purpose for your life Mathew 6:33, Proverb 3:5-6, Roman 6:1, 15.

First, let us state boldly and without equivocation that we hold to the Scriptures as being the Word of God. The written Word of Jehovah shall be intact, even; when the heavens and the earth pass away. The Scripture is the Word of God Almighty and we shall be judged by it in the Day of the Lord Revelation 20:12.

We have learned in this life that God will keep His Word and if there is any weakening of this promise, our faith is seriously undermined and without any doubt and or hesitations that would never happen – because, God gave us His Word in Rhema the spoken Word the

Mouth of God or Logos the written Word of His Eternal Holy Book 'The Bible' and we can depend on it 1 Corinthians 15:19.

We are not to be counted among those who attempt to analyse Bible, picking in random the Old Testament characters pointing to the mistakes of the patriarch and mix-match with New Testament experience and then make allowances for it by twisting what was written until it appears to be understandable and acceptable to the individual who desires to alter the Scriptures.

The Word of God is a joy to the saint and that he meditates therein day and night. However, we worship Christ and believe His Scriptures. We contend for the perfect accuracy and immutability of the written Word of God

Every son of God must learn to serve God while in the midst of his enemies. We must rule while surrounded by enemies, for it is there God sets a table for us. When our obedience has been perfected, God will remove Satan far from us. Even the memory of Satan will be banished forever from the mind of God's victorious saints. But the lessons of godliness we have learned as we have struggled against Satan are part of our character for eternity.

We do not need to twist the Word of God to suit our sinful desires and Pride because God Almighty the All Sufficient one would honour His Existence Psalm 138:2.

In this book, the subjects are treated in a straightforward way with simplicity. It is in language that all can understand with the confirmation of scriptural references and proven Personal testimonies.

When a believer is prepared to move in faith and obedience, God's best will be found. His love is always expressed in what He says and does.

Dear readers, are you willing to commit yourself to the leadings and teachings of the Holy Spirit through the written Word of God the Bible? He is able to give sound and scriptural advice 2Timothy 3:16. We just have to do everything He gives us the grace to do for Him in His divine ways; so that we will not Be I Know.

The book of Matthew 7:13-25 says Enter by the narrow gate; for the gate is wide and the way is easy, that leads to destruction, and those who enter by it are many. For the gate is narrow and the way is hard, that leads to life, and those who find it few. Beware of false prophets, who come to you in sheep's clothing but inwardly are ravenous wolves. You will know them by their fruits. Are grapes gathered from thorns or figs from thistles? So, every sound tree bears good fruit, but the bad tree bears evil fruit.

A sound tree cannot bear evil fruit, nor can a bad tree bear good fruit. Every tree that does not bear good fruit is cut down and thrown into the fire Revelation 20:15, 21:7-8. Thus you will know them by their fruits. Not everyone who says to me, 'Lord, Lord,' shall enter the kingdom of heaven, but he who does the will of my Father who is in heaven. On that day many will say to me, 'Lord, Lord, did we not prophesy in your name, and cast out demons in your name, and do many mighty works in your name?' And then will I declare to them, 'I never knew you; depart from me, you evildoers.' "Everyone then who hears these words of mine and does them will be like a wise man who built his house upon the rock, and the rain fell, and the floods came, and the winds blew and beat upon that house, but it did not fall, because it had been founded on the rock Deuteronomy 29:29, John 5:39.

Today like never before we must acknowledge and desire to seek God's plan for our lives, families, and our churches. God want to restore to us the fullness of original plan of His glory. But, we must be functioning according to His divine plans and blueprint not by our own and in so doing His divine Glory will come upon our lives 2 Chronicle 7:1, Exodus 40:33-38.

The cost of disobedience is too great; you might not able to afford it. Read 1 King 13:1-34 but I want us to concentrates on verses 20-25, Revelation 22:14-22.

GOD THE FATHER

In the Bible, we discover the three great levels of intelligent existence. The first and highest is Jehovah God Almighty or Jehovah Elohim, as in Blessed Godhead, the second are the Angels, and the third are humans (Psalms 8:4–6). (Please read all Scripture references throughout this text.)

God as Father, Son, and Holy Ghost, or we may say the Heavenly trio, as they are also called Elohim the Trinity. Through a number of Scriptures, we discover some of the physical aspects of God, like eyes to see, ears to hear, mouth to speak, and hands and feet to use. (Read 1 Peter 3:12.) We must be careful how literally we view this, as we must accept this Truth, especially about God, by faith (Hebrews 11:1, 6; Romans 1:17).

The power of insight is a right and a must for every true child of God for God cannot be explained, only be revealed. When the Spirit of God ask us to seek prophecy through one the counsel of the Apostle Paul, that it was a great gift because it comes into existence by means of revelatory Power Gifts, and a true prophecy through revelation gives birth to the gift of Discerning of spirits, of which every true Christian should seriously and earnestly confess (Proverbs 20:27, 1 Corinthians 2:11, Romans 8:14).

A human is not just a person because of physical aspects but because of certain characteristics that reveal what the human is like as a person. We see God is revealed in the Bible with personality traits, and thus we can imagine God as a person. In this book, we will refer to some of this personality trait of God. The first and foremost of this is love. "God is love," we read in 1 John 4:8. This love is revealed in what He has given to us (John 3:16 and 1 John 3:16).

In spite the fact that we humans have disobeyed God and deserve death, Romans 6:23 tells us that God still loves us immensely and shows that in what He has given to us. Now we have the opportunity to accept this gift for our salvation or reject it and be condemned. God challenges us to accept His divine gift in faith and be saved or reject His love and be condemned and perish (John 3:17–18).

God's love is also far different from what we humans call love. We love what we like and deem worthy to be loved, but God loved us before we showed any sign loving Him Read Romans 5:8. "God loved us when we were yet sinners" means that before we accepted Him as our Redeemer. After we come to God in faith, we may sin, but He is always there to forgive us (1 John 1:9).

When Moses desired to see God, the Lord answered, "No one can see me and live" (Exodus 33:20). However, God revealed His character to Moses in Exodus 34:6–7. These attributes are similar to what we find in Exodus 20:6. For that reason, the Ten Commandments are also considered a transcript of God's character. We read in Exodus 20:5 that God is a jealous God, not jealous like humans can be because that is a sin, but that God does not allow any worship or honor given to something or someone besides Him. The third and the fourth commandments remind us of His holiness. God is Holy, His name is Holy, and His day is Holy. The other six commandments remind us that God is a caring God. He created us humans being and we ought to respect each other because we are all His creatures (Romans 12:10 1 Peter 1:22; 2:17).

In the book of Psalms, we find a number of things about God and what He is like. God is a shield, protecting and guarding us (Psalms 33:20; 28:7; 119:114). Sometimes it may look like God is not shielding us, but here again, as I mentioned, in the beginning, earlier, we have to learn to live by faith. One day it will be revealed why it seems that He did not shield us in certain situations and circumstances.

God is also a God who knows the end from the beginning (Isaiah 44:6–7 and 45:8, 10). We have to trust God as all-wise and who knows best what to do, what to allow, and what to prevent. Some of Christ's disciples had difficulty believing when not seeing, as in the case of Thomas, which you can read in John 20:27–29. When Christ revealed Himself to Thomas, in shame Thomas fell down before Christ and said, "My Lord and my God," and Jesus said, "Blessed are those who are not seeing but believing" That's what we should be, trusting the all-wise and Almighty God, because He has created us and because when we were still sinners He loved us and gave His Son, Jesus Christ, to redeem us from sin.

But let's go back to the psalms and learn more about God. God is also a rock, solid and firm, that can be trusted without fail (Psalms 18:2; 42:9; 95:1). God is also a king, which reveals His royalty and majesty (Psalms 44:4; 74:12). He is the sovereign God of the universe that He has created and as such asks us to remember His day (Exod. 20:8–11) and worship Him (Revelation 14:6–7). Then God is also our shepherd, which is beautifully explained in Psalm 23 (read all of it) and 80:1. David was a shepherd, so he knew what a shepherd is like, and God is the same for us as our shepherd. God is also our refuge; in times of trouble, we know where to go for safety, comfort, and divine sympathy and empathy (Psalms 46:1; 62:7). God is also the great deliverer and redeemer (Psalms 18:2; 37:39–40), which means He is our Savior (Psalms107:2; read also Isaiah 43:1, 11, 14; 44:6). But God is also a judge who will judge the world in righteousness (Psalms 96:13; Revelations15:3; 16:5 20:12). And much more is revealed in the Scriptures and in nature about the divine Godhead and their counsel. You will find and discover that when you read the Bible yourself.

My Personal Testimonies about God

In 1988, I was in the spirit and saw myself caught up in the middle of heaven. A scroll rolled down, and I was able to read two lines, which I vividly remember. They read, "Eyin ni Eleri Mi," which means in English, "Ye are my witnesses." I then woke up.

Also in 1988, one night I had a vision that I was walking along the beach with Jesus Christ. The picture I saw was like the portrait in the Bible story, as we were walking together on the pure white sand. As we went along, I discovered two sets of footprints but along the line, I did not see Him by my side again On awakening, I saw only one set of footprints and myself. Whenever He calls me He says my Native name, Olubunmi.

Again in 1988, I woke up and prepared to go to school with my two younger sisters. We were in a hurry to catch the train, which was about twenty to thirty minutes away. I thought it was the 6:00 a.m. train I did not know a train called Limited was passing a few minutes before 2:00 a.m. God Almighty, who neither slumbers nor sleep, saw me that very day. As I was about to lead my two sisters out of our house, I immediately heard His voice call, "Olubunmi, go back!" I instantly obeyed because I know His voice. It was the same voice I was familiar with in previous communications, and on two or three occasions when He appeared to me in the spirit, His image was a full figure and mighty man sitting in an armchair in heaven. In each instance, inside heaven, do part open on accord?

Dear friend, are you willing to commit yourself to the Creator of the universe? Almighty God, Jehovah is His name. Make Him the centre of your life, worship Him, and give Him glory. Are you willing to love God as He loves you? I strongly believe and I want you to believe that Jehovah God is *real* (Psalm 24).

JESUS CHRIST

The Anointed One and Son of God

Jesus Christ is the Son of God and the second person of the Trinity We must start with John 1:1–3. To understand this passage clearly, we will analyze it point by point.

"In the beginning was the Word." We learn from Genesis 1 that God used His voice and His Word to create and to bring things into being. For each of the six creation days, we read, "And God said." This is confirmed in Psalm 33:6 in the Word of God. In verse 9, we read, "He spoke and commanded ..." God's voice and His word were used in the creation.

The next point in John 1:1 is that "the Word was with God." In other words, the Word was with the heavenly trio—God—from the beginning. In a moment we will discover who that Word is.

The third point that we find in verse 1 is that "the Word was God" It was divine in nature. In verse 2, we learn that "the same"—the Word—"was in the beginning with God," that is with the heavenly trio. Then verse 3 reveals that "by Him"—that is, the Word—"all things were made and without Him was not anything made that was made." It is clear from these passages that the Word created all things.

The logical question to ask is "Who is John talking about?" To answer that question, we have to read further in John 1 to verse 14, which says, "The Word was made flesh and dwelt among us (and we beheld His glory, the glory as of the only-begotten of the Father) full of grace and truth." Let's examine this also point by point. The Word was made flesh. Who is it that was made flesh? Rom.8:3 have the answer. We read "that God has sent His own son in the likeness of sinful flesh." This means the Son of God, Jesus incarnated. He was and still is divine nature and glory and became flesh. Sinful flesh does not mean he was a sinner, Jesus never sinned (2 Cor.5:21) but he had a human body with the effects of sin, he needed food, he could be weak, in need of sleep and more could be mentioned.

In Gal.4:4 we read that God sent forth His Son (Jesus Christ) born of a woman (Mary) in human flesh.

The next point is the Word which was made flesh dwelt among us. In John 14:8 Philip asks the question of Jesus, "show us the Father" and Jesus answers "Have I been so long time with you and yet hast thou not known me; Philip"? Jesus is the one who was made flesh and dwelt among us, the following point in John 1:14 are "we beheld His glory." Often Glory in the Bible stands for character, God's character which is also revealed in His name. In Exod.33:13 Moses asked that God would show Himself to him. The answer is in Ex.33:21, 22. God's Glory would pass and when it passed in Ex.34:6, 7 the Lord proclaimed His character. In Rev.18:1 we read that the earth will be lightened with God's Glory or the knowledge of God. Read Isa. 11:9 and Isa.60:1, 2 A messages will go around the globe, planet earth, to reveal who God is. His name will be proclaimed and in that name, His character will be made known.

The powers of darkness Satan, give the wrong picture of God; so God will make sure that a message goes around which will give a true picture of God, who He is; and that will be revealed in Christ and His followers. Jesus Christ birth was revealed right from the time of the Prophets and Kings Isaiah 6: 9. Psalms 110:1 Psalm 8:6, Proverb 8.

As sinners, we lost the glory of God; we had before the fall in Eden Rom.3:23. Therefore we have to be born again, become a new creature in Christ and have the glory of God restored in us, John 3:1-5; 2 Cor.5:17 Baptism through water and the Spirit is the spiritual testimonies of being born again Acts 8:26-40. Once again I tell you, believe me; this is the Major and Primary step in fulfilling your destiny and God's purpose for your life on this earth John 14:6, 15:1-7, Act 4:12.

The next point in John 1:14 is the glory was seen in the Word, in Jesus, "as of the only begotten of the Father." This raises another question? Was Jesus begotten or born as we are? Yes, we all know the story; as a human child of Mary he was born as we are, but not because Mary had been with a man; Jesus was conceived by the Holy Spirit, Matt.1:20 and also read Luke 1:35 Jesus would be called the Son of God, not the son of Joseph, Mary's husband, this is confirmed in Proverbs 8:23-31.

So what does it mean then to be begotten of the Father? We read the same in John 3:16 "His only begotten Son." It means His unique Son, someone special, we may even say very special. That's why Jesus only could reveal the father, His glory, and character and that's why he could say to Philip, "if you have seen me, you have seen the Father." John 14:9. The names predicted about Jesus in Isa.9:6 also clearly do indicate who Jesus is, "the mighty God"

We go to the next point, "full of grace and truth." In Titus 2:11 we read about the grace of God. God's grace is revealed in Jesus Christ and therefore the Bible also speaks of the "grace of our Lord Jesus Christ" 1 Cor.16:23.

In the gift of Jesus, from God (John3:16) we receive grace, in other words, Christ to us is God's gift of grace. But what about "truth" In Jesus also Truth is revealed. He is the self-declared TRUTH, John 14:6. He had a delight in the law and came to magnify the law, Ps.40:8; Isa.42:21. And God's law and commandments are the truth, Ps.119:142, 151.

We conclude at this point that the Word John writes about here in John 1:1-3 is Jesus Christ who was with God in the beginning. And we read in Genesis.1:1. We confirm also that in or through Jesus all has been made, which qualifies Jesus for being the Creator, Colossians 1:16, Proverbs 8:23-31.

We will underline the point that Jesus is God, as it reads here in John 1:1" the Word was God." Yes, Jesus is as much God, as He is human like you and me. Turn to Hebrews 1 and we find God talking about His Son.

The author of the Hebrews has God talking and making a clear difference between the angels, who are ministers, and Jesus who is God. Read Hebrew 1:7, 8. The obvious conclusion is that; to none of the angels God was declared His Son, but of Jesus Christ God declared that He is His Son, Matt.3:17; Luke 3:22. Then in Hebrew.1:6 we read that God says "let all the angels of God worship Him." Only the divine being, is due to receive proper worship, not angels. Read Rev.19:10; 22:8, 9 angels refused to be worshipped when John felt down in an act of worship. But Jesus receives worship, Rev. 4:10, 11; 5:14; 19:4. The last book of the Bible is the Revelation of Jesus Christ. Moreover, we read in Hebrew.1:8-9 the anointed Christ. Yes, Jesus is fully God, Son of God, but also fully man, Son of Man. He is the Creator and He has been created, incarnated in the womb of Mary WITHOUT NATURAL CONCEPTION.

My personal testimonies about Jesus Christ

First of these, was the insight about the footprints I pen down at the beginning of this book and whenever I hear my First name I know is the one calling me or talking to me and or if He appears to me; just as a young as a figure of a Man.

I remember an insight, sometime in1989, I saw a woman offering sacrifice to demon of Molech and she was crawling moving towards my room, I quickly got up and slammed the door against her and therefore, immediately I saw Christ appeared (The same Picture of Him as in the Footprint) walking around my entire house and I was singing with my two sisters these children Sunday school song we normally sing:

Jesus is passing this way ... 3x

Jesus is passing this way,

He is passing this way today.

The Lord Saviour Jesus Christ always watching over us – He never sleeps nor slumber and even He is always at the right hand's sides of God Almighty pleading on our behalf Psalm 121:1-5, Roman 8:34

Another experience was with one of my daddies in the Lord who was a minister of God and I saw that some men who we were familiar with and that we could have call elder and friends were seriously hitting him with big firewood to the extent he fell on ground but to my surprise Jesus Christ (The same Picture of Him as in the Footprint) came out of bush like a meadow and hits them back with Iron and I woke up.

Another privilege night was when I found myself kneeling in a Large Congregation of Saints, I saw Christ Jesus, and He laid His hand on me and prayed for me.

Dear friend, Jesus Christ is real and He is always available to make Himself known to us with the portrait and way we can understand.- He watches over us and protects us from all kinds of evil men as I had mentioned above

HOLY SPIRIT

This Chapter expands about the third "Person" of the Godhead, the Holy being of The Heavenly Trio. I put a person in quotation marks because the Holy Spirit is a person of a different substance than God the Father or the Son of God, Jesus Christ.

To start giving us a picture of the Holy Spirit, we will do again as we did in the previous Chapters and go back to the beginning. We will do that more often with other future subjects as well. In Genesis 1:2, we find that the Spirit of God, which is the Holy Spirit, was moving upon the waters at the time of creation. The Holy Spirit had a part in the creation with the other two members of the Godhead or The Heavenly Trio.

The Hebrew word in Genesis chapter one for God is 'Elohim' a plural word. It shows that what we understand as God is a complex word and plural. God is one but revealed in three different ways, Father, Son and Holy Spirit, Matth.28:19. At creation, the Father, Son, and Holy Spirit worked together as God to get the creation done.

The next time we meet the Spirit is in Gen.6:3 where He said 'My Spirit shall strive not always with man'. 'Strive' means, to plead with a man, pleading to get a man to turn from his wicked ways, trying to convert them, to make a turnaround. Jesus later spoke about the same kind of work of the Holy Spirit in John16:8 to reprove or convince of sin, righteousness, and judgment. People often think that the Holy Spirit only played a role in New Testament Times, but we find that the Holy Spirit has always been present right from the beginning.

Let's read a few more from the Old Testament times. Gen.41:38 Pharaoh recognized that Joseph was filled with the Spirit of God and had the wisdom to help Egypt through times of famine.

Then in Exodus 31:2-3 Bezaleel was called to be the builder of the sanctuary in the desert and was filled with the Spirit of God, with wisdom to do the building.

We find also that kings could be filled with God's Spirit. 1 Sam.11:6 the Spirit of God upon King Saul. Then the king, or king to be, David in 1 Sam.16:13. But at the same time King Saul lost the Spirit of God, 1 Sam.16:14, because of his transgression, refusal to obey God. It also means we can lose the guidance of the Holy Spirit if we fall into apostasy or if we turn our back to God, neglect his divine Words, directive principle, and pattern as King Saul did. We read a similar warning from the apostle Paul in 2 Thess.2:11. If people reject the truth, God will send them other spirits.

In the time of the judges, we find the Spirit of God active. Judg.3:10; 6:34. Prophet of the OT speaks about the Spirit of God in Isa. 11:2; 48:16; 61:1. When David had sinned he prayed to God not to take away from him the Holy Spirit, read Ps.51:11. Apparently, David knew what had happened to King Saul and he did not want the same to happen to him.

What do we know about the functions of the Holy Spirit? Read again Isa.11:2 the Spirit of God grants us wisdom, understanding of problems, counsel when we need. When we are in situations not knowing what to do, the Holy Spirit will be our guide. The Holy Spirit also is expressed in terms of Might and Strength. He empowers us. In Daniel, we read several times that he was filled with the Spirit of God and able to assist the kings of Babylon in their dilemma and frustrations. Dan.2:9; 5:11.

Jesus spoke about the Holy Spirit and gives us some more information about the activities of the Holy Spirit. I have already mentioned John 16:8, but in 16:13 we read more. The Holy Spirit will guide in all truth and in John 17:17 we find that God's Word is truth. This is very important. Many so-called Christians claim to have the Holy Spirit but their teachings are not in harmony with the Word of God. The Holy Spirit never leads or guides us outside the written Word of God, the Bible. The Holy Spirit is invisible by His nature, but the Word of God, the Bible is clear and visible for our guide and direction. Never accept anything from a so-called spirit filled people when their teachings are not in harmony with the Bible, the Word of God. Always ask for a reference to the Holy Scriptures, the Bible. Jesus defended Himself against the temptation of the Devil by using the scriptures. Jesus said "It is written," read Matth.4:4, 7 and 10

When Jesus said that the Holy Spirit will convince us of sin, the Word of God in 1 John 3:4 tells us that sin is the transgression of God's law. If people have no regard for the law of God or willfully and decidedly transgress God's law, we may know that they have not the Holy Spirit. Read Acts 5:32 the Holy Spirit is given to people who obey God. Also in Isaiah 8:20 say; if they do not speak of the law and testimony they have no light. The laws are the Bible (LOGOS) written and the testimony (RHEMA) is what comes out of the mouth of God, Ps.119:88. If people claim to have the Spirit of God you must test their teachings with the Word of God 1John 5:8, 2 Corinthians 3:6.

In Joel 2:28 we read that God will give His spirit to old and young and they will prophesy, which means they will be filled with divine Spiritual experience and relay what they have received from God through His Word read also 2 Peter 1:21. Holy men of God moved by the Holy Ghost and It should be clear that when any person has the privileges of receiving divine revelation he or she is under a solemn obligation to be faithful at relaying divine messages accurately Act 26:19, Revelation 22:18-19.

After Jesus had ascended into the heavens, ten days later a special outpouring of the Holy Spirit took place empowering the initial preaching of the message of Christ, His death, and resurrection. Acts.2:1-3. Their message was heard in different languages which the apostles had not learned beforehand …

In the beginning of this Chapter, I mentioned that the Holy Spirit is a "Person," because of personality and characteristics He portrays. As humans, we often look to ourselves when we speak about a person, but when we speak about heavenly things that are different they are not the same as the earthly. The personality of the holy being or the Heavenly Trio cannot be compared with the personality of humans. We speak about God the father as a Person, because of what is revealed about Him; we speak about Jesus, the Son of God, as a Person as He has been revealed in the Word of God. Even after Christ's resurrection Jesus acted as a person, but different from us, in a different substance, He was not subject to distance and material matters. So is the Holy Spirit also a Person, but different in substance. In other words, it should be clear that only the spirit and soul of Man make a man a real being and not necessary a body; you cannot know a man by physical appearance except by what is inside of him (spirit or soul). A body was given to enable man to feel, touch and stay on earth that is why you see a spirit always looking for a body to use whenever in operation and if they did not see they use that of animals to possess Mark 1:21-26, 5:7-13. In Acts 5:1-4 we find that Peter accuses Ananias of having lied against the Holy Ghost, which Peter calls in the last part of verse 4, God. We can only lie against a person.

In John 14:26 Jesus presents the Holy Spirit as a teacher another indication of a personality, and in John 16:13 as a guide In Acts 13:2 the Holy Spirit gives instruction about what to do, and in Acts 16:6,

7 where to go. From Acts 20:28 we learn that the Holy Spirit acted in placing overseers, Ministers in the church. In Rom.8:26 the Holy Spirit directs our prayer. We read in Mattew.12:31 that it is possible to speak against the Holy Spirit which means to resist His influence upon us. Also in Acts 7:51 when we speak about God as Father, Son, and Holy Spirit we establish the fact that God is omnipotent which means Almighty, 2 Cor.6:18; Rev.21:22; God is also omniscient, God knows everything nothing is hidden from Him, Deut.30:11; Ps.139:1-4, and God is also omnipresent, we cannot hide away from God, Ps.139:7-9. For God being everywhere takes place through the third person of the Godhead, the Holy Spirit. God is everywhere at the same time and in that manner God speaks to everyone who is willing to listen and receive the things which the Holy Spirit gets from God; John 16:13, 14. We conclude that being omnipotent, omniscient and omnipresent applies to God, Father, Son, and Holy Spirit inclusive.

God the Father, God the Son and God the Holy Spirit are one in all and divers in operations. In these three we are baptized, Matth.28:19 and receive divine blessing 2 Cor.13:14.

My personal testimonies about the Holy Spirit:

I speak in Truth; I was privileged to receive from the blessed third person of the Godhead; divine Spirit of God in many ways, situations, and circumstances. In many instances, for those of us familiar with Him, He just comes by like a drop of a pin in the ocean. In some occasion He appears as per interpreting Him as an Elderly or Mature physical man of God; to give instruction, information, and warning.

If I should start giving an account of His relationship with me; you will be wondering and at the same time want to doubt if someone like me could have all these kind of divine experience.

The first one I remembered to share with us was when I was age Seven (7) He made me see vividly that someone can carry another close friend face but not the entire body. One night in 1978, I was lying on my bed, when I saw some group of women ties white cloth singing and dancing at the front of the staircase of another tenant frontage in the house myself and family stayed in one of the populous Cities. On my bed I saw them calling my name first time, second time and third time I did not answer them and their leader turned as if she want to look toward where I was lying on my bed and I discovered that it was the face of a woman I know and instantly they all raised their hand to give me obeisance. At the second day her mother put the face of my close childhood friend's mother to lured me to her side, my friend mother appeared from another angle and was calling me and telling me that she was the real person of this my friend mother (I decided not to mention my friend name), not the first woman, how I got to know the first woman was my landlady was that; my friend mother was not as big and fat like my landlady, she only succeeded in picking her face not her body. I had the same experience 1994 where a sister picked another sister friend face to deceived me in following her to somewhere; I said No, no; this is sister B, not sister A, I know instantly, even the way this sister B walk in my insight was different from the way sister A walk physically and this particular sister B also came to me in the spirit realm few year later when we meet on narrow bridge where the under was an endless dungeon she was coming to push me into that dungeon I quickly pushed her inside and after few years she died mysteriously (not that I am happy about this; but to let us know that we cannot deceive the Spirit of God). We can see here that Holy Spirit of Christ reveal to warn the kind of so-called friends and associates we keep

In 1981 at 1:45am at the awakening of a morning I saw in the spirit that my immediate sister fell into a well; this is another house the same Lagos; I got up in the middle of that night and started praying; somehow from my young age I learned to return evil back to sender, so I prayed this simple prayer that night 'if I see anybody that want to throw my sister inside well, let it be that is their children that shall fall inside well' and to my surprise; that morning before noon of the day of that night it was one woman staying in the shop at the front of my flat had her son fell inside well. After that incident if I am coming and the woman also was coming, she quickly diverted to the other side of the road removed her face to the other side and quickly pass. I was just thinking about this woman reactions because it is like what someone else would say it just ordinary dream of the night but yet; the woman reacts as if there were physical contacts, and It was not too long she back out to another place - Thanks to divine Spirit of God.

Another incident of like these was when Holy Spirit open my eyes to see a large conference in the Satanic domain they were seriously deliberating that they do not want Pa/Prophet T. Obadare to lead Christ Apostolic Church they do not just want him few of the member of this group were sitting on high stools, they were many and most of us reading this book know what happened - the Church of God that could have united in strong Prophetic Anointing and missions divided and it became "back to your Tent o Israel"

What I am trying to portrait here was that Divine Sprit of God give accurate information's, instruction and warning: what need to be, what is going on around you and how it happen or must have happened and or reason something is not happening 1 Samuel 8:4-9 and 19-21.

The other experience I had was when I was in higher institution, when God open my eyes to see one of my roommates that had dual personalities of Lion and Snake and truly in the physical, she confesses to such effects that she has twelve snakes with the golden cobra among them and this particular golden cobra was used to chastise her whenever she makes love Tuesdays and Thursdays. She confesses this after one day like that; when I was very hungry for five days I do not have anything to eat; is like she notices this; she dresses like a Christian sister and brought me food in the spirit, I rushed the food to the extent I licked the plate clean. As soon as I finished eating the Eba and Ogbono soup I heard the gentle Holy Spirit and He called on me and said "Child you just finish eating in the dream," because the experience I had that day was like I sat up on my spring bed as if the experience was physical and real. Immediately I heard the Spirit of God telling me this; trust me, my normal way of prayer in a situation like this: I pray; 'every target and consequence of this food, back to the sender in Sevenfold'. And so it happened that she was diagnosed with a very a big acute boil and was hospitalised for three months and three weeks and also, she missed educational sections for that year.

Divine Spirit of God is the exposer of all secrets especially to His own, He is the number one and excellent security anyone could have and that could give accurate Information. And more also, without Holy Spirit no mortal man will able to raise from dead not to talk of meeting Christ in the sky when He returns 1Thessalonians 4:17, Ephesians 2:1, Roman 8:9,11, Revelation 11:12.

Dear friends, you need to seek Him – Holy Spirit of God with all your heart Jeremiah 29:13, Amos 5:4, Matthew 7:7-10.

THE BIBLE

The Bible messages are eternal as God, Christ, and the Holy Spirit are eternal; it reveals to us God's everlasting covenant and plan of salvation … Books have come and gone over thousands of years, the Bible still is, because it comes from the Great I am, who still is and will be.

"No book has been so loved, so hated, and so revered and or neglected as the Bible. People have died for it. Others have been killed for it, sometimes I even wonder why people ever ready and always claim good parts of the bible and reject or try to twist it in other too easy their fallen nature and ego 2 Peter 3:15-16. Today there is no language in the civilized world unto which this Word of God has not been rendered

The Bible is God's unfailing inspired Word, transmitted in human language. The Bible is God's absolute and certain truth for a fragmented uncertain world. The Bible is God's mind in human language for our human mind. The Bible is God's thinking communicated to men Psalm 119:89, Matthew 24:35

The Bible is world's bestselling book, most translated, oldest in age, but also world's most misunderstood, misapplied in many parts of the world and the least read.

The Bible reveals the past, guides us through the present, and prepares us for the future. It gives Basic Information before leaving this Earth, many people, when condemned to a solitary confined place, would choose to take the Bible if so allowed, and many people in dying hours in need of comfort would rather hear a word from the Bible than from any other piece of literature.

The Bible is: comfort to the mourner, healing to the sick, joy to the glad, wisdom to the student, salvation to the sinner, condemnation to the wicked, history to the historian, poetry to the poet, security to the fearful, hope to the one in despair, treasure to the value seeker, resurrection to the one meeting death, vision to the one disillusioned, power to the weak, strength to the one discouraged, food for the hungry, drink to the thirsty, justice to the maltreated.

As said before, mankind has tried to fight the Bible: In the dark ages it was a forbidden book; even possessing a Bible could bring someone on the stake and be burned to death. Some kingdom launched a strong campaign against the Bible but soon found out that it failed. In modern day history for 70 years during the 20th century, the teachings of some sects have tried to silence the voice of the Bible but also to no avail. Also, in our present generation, we have heard a situation where several occasions commands go forth to sink a big ship full of bibles in the Sea.

HOW DOES THE BIBLE DESCRIBE ITSELF?

I am a lamp for your feet, Ps.119:105, I am a light on your path, I am the book of the Lord, Isa.34:16, I am the Gospel of God, Rom.1:1, I am the oracles of God, Rom.3:2

I am the Word of God, Hebr.6:5, I am the Word of Christ, Col.3:16, I am the Word that stands forever, Isa.40:8, I am very pure, Ps.119:140, I am like fire, Jer.23:29, I am like sweet honey, Ezek.3:3, I am sometimes sweet in the mouth, bitter in the stomach, Rev.10:9, I am a comfort in affliction, Ps.119:30, I am the Truth, John 17:17, I am joy to those eating me, Jer.15:16, I am the sword of the Spirit, Eph.6:17, I am a two-edged sword, Hebr.4:12, I am eternal life to those searching me, John 5:39, I am divinely inspired, God-breathed and profitable for doctrines, reproof, correction, instruction, 2 Tim.3:16, I am more than all this, but I am all that man needs, can hope for and be fully satisfied with.

PERSONAL TESTIMONIES ABOUT THE WORD - BIBLE

Do you know what? God still referred back to what was written in the bible. For example in one of my personal relationship with Him some years back in 1999/2000, I sat at the front of my room in one of those well-established oil Company Residential quarters. I was reading one of these Rick Joyner's books; and not up to 10minutes I was caught up, everything around me became invisible and I was more spiritually conscious. Then I heard Father the Creator of Heaven and Earth (Jehovah) speaks. This is our conversation:-

God: How many people did I save during the time of Noah?
Me: I answer Daddy is Eight (8).
God: He said Fine.
God: How many did I save during the time of Sodom and Gomorrah?
Me: I answer 4 people, but the wife; as I was trying to explain.
God: He caught me short, instantly and said –

WHAT DID PEOPLE TAKE ME FOR?

You can see now that even God referred back to scripture He empowered and use men to put down as His mind into words for us 'as per Bible', and immediately that very day after this conversation I ran inside my room I felt I should pick my bible and the first place I open on random was Luke 17:26 and read through 32.

The men God use to writes Bible were been guided a right and there is no Mistake in all God uses them to gathered and pen down in the Bible 2 Timothy 3:16, Genesis 6:1-22. Also, Christ defeats Satan by simply referring him back to what scriptures had said. Matt 4:7, Luke 4:8. Even satan that deceives the heart of men to denial the infallible of the bible also quote the scripture Luke 4:10-11,

The Bible is viewed as the source of objective truth. It is authoritative in all areas of our lives. From the Bible, the believer can draw application for living a godly life. From the Bible, the believer understands who God is, what He does and has done, and how to have a personal relationship with Him through faith in the Lord Jesus Christ. If any man preaches or teach any other gospel than that which Paul proclaimed, he is to be accursed Gal. 1:8-9, 12, 1Thess. 2:13, 1Cor. 14:37, how much more the whole truth in Bible God Himself Stamped and Signed with His breath Matthew 5:18. The holy Bible is a book of life that will be open along with other Books on the Judgment day Daniel 7:10, Revelation 11:18, 20:12-15.

ANGEL

The heavenly angels are beings living with God in heaven, they are different from humans, and they are often referred to as guardian angels, They Come as a result of prayer and belief and we do see them in Dreams, In Visions, and in Person. Matthew 1:20, Daniel 10:5-6, 7, they were mentioned numerous times in the Scriptures. In the account of the Scripture, we learn that angels are spiritual beings created by God to serve Him, and sent by God to watch over the human race, to deliver His message, to guard and protect us from danger, to do battle with other spiritual beings on our behalf. Though, we are commanded by God not to worship them as this is blasphemy. Colossians 2:18, Revelation 19:10; 22:9.

Since the beginning of time, angels have delivered God's messages to mankind. Sometimes the messages are warnings of impending danger, sometimes instructions as to what to do in a particular situation, sometimes they are simply "there" as protection from enemy forces. Sometimes they bring joyful announcements as in the day they announced the birth of Jesus. Luke 1:11, Acts 8:26-29, Hebrews 1:13-14, 1st Kings 19:5, Acts 5:17-21, Exodus 33:2, Psalm 91:11-12, Matthew 13:41-42

In truth, God can deal with us in any way that pleases Him. He can speak with us directly, in a burning bush, in dreams, visions and specifically through the Scriptures. Yet, he also employs angels. The

Scripture says angels were created for His pleasure. Perhaps it is as simple as that -- it pleases God to send the supernatural heavenly beings we call "angels" to minister to his children.

The first place they are mention was in the Garden of Eden prevent Adam and Eve getting to the tree of life. Cherubim were placed at the entrance, Gen.3:22. Cherubim are the name for one group of angels. The other group we find named in Isaiah .6:2, 6, are under the name of Seraphim, these have 6 wings; they are the nearest to the throne of God. Good angels are ministers or messengers, unseen to us, but very real and have been experienced by people in the past and the present as well.

The name angel is from the Greek word Angelo They minister unto God and unto men, Dan.7:10; Hebr.1:14. The name means messenger. One of their trait I found out was that they asked you question as if they want to be sure of what they are sent to do at a particular time.

Personal Testimonies on Angel:

I remember when I was like 9 years old, I was on holiday in the place of one of my old ones in the village, and anytime I went there the whole community will bring whatever they had for me to eat, but my old one will not allow me to eat any food brought; and it does worry me. One particular day, my old one had to go to farm and she decided to take me along to fetch firewood; I have been to this place more than four times, then it was about to go for the last time on the same trips of fetching firewood from the farm to the compound on that very day, I lost my way home and found myself just walking and lost in the bush, only me going I do not know where I was going I just keep going, and around after Six with only me in the Forest. It got to a point in that forest I heard someone talking to me on top of very high tree he was on red top and trouser with face cap, no shoe he was standing straight on top of the tree, he asked me 'Are you' Olubunmi and I answered,' Yes', he then told me "take this way and go straight". I obeyed and came to the main road within a short trek. The whole communities have come out scattered looking for me. When I came out to the main road I had to trek a long distance before I could get back to my own community. My old ones were already crying, asking the question of who they had offended. It was getting dark when I got home and they were just asking me questions and I explained all that happened. Then one of the sympathizers a chief hunter of the place said that the incident happens because I come across a Leaf called "MU Ode Sina – meaning a leaf that makes the hunter miss his way and it is used by witches for misleading and frustrations. And I was told that if I should not have received the ministry of that Angel; I would have gotten to one dangerous inviting river, and then only God could have known what might have happened.

In 1990, I received another tremendous ministry of Angels on one particular day like that. I was hungry and I decided to go to one of my Aunt and friends at a PLACE CALLED Oke Aro Lagos. As soon as I got to one junction a song came to my spirit it was Evangelist Ebenezer Obey song that says Mo jade loni Eledumare 2x Ji jade mi ki ma Pade Agbako, Ohun Maje Ni Mo Nwalo Baba, Maje Npade Oun Ti Oje Mi- meaning I am going today O Lord 2x let my going out be without evil befalling me, I am going to look for what I will eat do not let me meet what will eat me. As the song came I just sang it out, is not up to some few minute I came to the middle of the wide un-tarred road called Waterworks road, the only thing I saw at my front was a lady with a keg of water suddenly diverted with terrible fear into a meadow and I was like asking myself 'what is wrong with her or did I look like her creditor? At the same time I just turned and look my back Lo and behold many angry Cows; they were like pursuing me to the extent the Hausa man in charge of them fear and lost control, he was trying to stop them, but it was like the way I saw them that day all the cows eyes were red and I could see and sense their anger, what would I do, the road was so wide that there was no place to run and hide that they will not meet me up and there was no enough stamina in me to run ahead of those Cows. So, I gather strength and I started running anyway; and the cow were seriously pursuing; suddenly at the middle of that same road I just saw an old modern Beatle Car- called Yeri Npeto meaning remove your head let me spite; two men were inside, one was driving the other one sat at back and open down the front door wide for me; when I finally ran toward them they beckoned on me and said I should quickly enter, without hesitation I entered and they zoom off. We just decided to look back and behold what we saw was that instantly the entire Cow turned back. The two men in the car then asked me which way I was going and I told them to the right that they should just stop me at the junction and I will find my way, they stopped me and I thanked them, I just said within me to turn back Lo and Behold both the Car and the Men disappear I did not see them again.

Another one was the day I was going to submit my Research Project on Campus, right from the house there was a contemplation in my mind either to pass Oshodi or Iyana Ipaja, finally, I decided to go through Iyana Ipaja. The money I had on me could not even take me through Oshodi to Badary, therefore, I decided to pass through Iyana Ipaja thinking that I will see help along the way so that I can use the remaining money to go and come back as planned. As I was standing I saw a car packed and I asked the driver if they can help me to LASU, I shouldn't have asked because they were three young men; though they do not even answer me so I just stood there, it was not up to five-minute I heard action and a very young teenage boy with a gun named double barrels and my first time to sight such a gun came out and start firing, to the faithfulness of God I do not know how I was carried from the side of their vehicle and drop under a shop with a distance to the main road and I was sure I did not run. It then occurs to me that I asked help from the assassins, It was later when I was going that I saw the man they came for; he was shot dead with one innocent shop assistant and others were injured.

As mentioned before; the Ministry of Angels is real and their ministration is to advance the Glory of the Divine Godhead in the Life of His People. Angels are all individually created and they do not marry and have no gender, Matth.22:30; Mark 12:25. Like the one that came to give me a message one time like that around 1994 was like a female; and he said; 'The Lord your God asked me to tell you, you are His witnesses confirming the message of God Himself to me as I have indicated in the early chapter of this book and as I remember, the second message it was like judgments to certain people around me'. Like humans, Angels have the power of free choice, to choose to do right or wrong, many who choose to do wrong are now kept until the time of their judgment, Jude 1:6, in that day to come they will be destroyed like Sodom and Gomorrah., Jude 1:7.

In other words, there are two types of angels; the good ones and evil ones Matthew 25:41, Daniel 10:12-14, 2 Corinthians 11:13-15 The evil angels are those angels that fell along with the Lucifer when he became arrogant in heaven, God drove them away to the earth Isaiah 14:12-15, Revelation 12:7-10 and on the planet Earth they established their own hierarchy and kingdom of which comprises of principality, power, ruler of darkness and wicked spirit in high places Ephesians 6:12. They are many in number they are legion and sometimes they paraded themselves as Angel of light 2 Corinthians 11:14; they are very intelligent and skilful and also pretenders in the form of human agent Luke 16:8. They are to steal, kill and destroyed every good thing God creates for all His creatures Genesis 1:31, 1Timothy 4:4, these four major fallen angels have numerous fallen spirit called demon working for them and array under them and some of these demons are:-

Asmodeus: this particular demon is in charge of all kind of sexual perversions and pollution. The demon Jezebel work under him, she makes use of both males and most especially females into harlotry, prostitutions, fornication in order to seduce weak men. I remember in one of the night, the Spirit of God gave me insight in 1997/1998 and 2006, the first one I saw was that some ladies were on white wrappers dancing in circle and they were singing like this Iya ni ya nje o 4x Awon oniya meta gba ominira, okunrin to ba ti dowo won o.. araiye abake – abake, which means that 'Mother a great mother 4x they are of three cords kind of mother, now they have gained their freedom any man that fall into their hands/trap the whole wide world will cry with him. The second one was I saw a so call Christian choir mistress of her church in a leading group of many unfamiliar ladies in conference with their queen mother in the middle and she was asking their queen (a familiar deaconess face, though, not married) and she said; 'queen give us permission to go and turn the heart of all Ministers, and their queen said Go … … … And I woke up. Please do not misquote me not all choir mistresses.

Sometimes it amazed me why sexual sin so terrible and deeper in mystery with Godhead than what anybody could imagine, no wonder God declared in His word that let every man should drink from his own cistern Proverb 5:15, 1 Corinthians 7:2.

In one of the unpleasant testimonies in the Faith many years; I was told how one of jezebel daughter, planned to fall a man of God many years back in Ibadan. A man full of strengths, anointing and powers of many privileges and Grace, I learnt that angels did cut his hair when full, this angel of darkness and daughter of jezebel and serpent went on top of one of Ibadan prayer mountain and fast for 21 days in order to get this man of God into a sexual sin; and that was the end of all the man's Powers and Grace

In 1993, I went to visit some of my Christian sisters and I heard some Physical Spiritual experience from them of how a young lady was arrested by the divine Spirit of God in one of the campus Crusade, this lady had slept with many young men of which those men will never make it or prosper again in life, except the last one she slept with that have not got her sperm to their reservoir, she mention the guy's name and they quickly get in the library hurled him down to crusade ground for deliverance that was the only young man that escaped her atrocities on men. You see how young men put themselves into everlasting agonies and they turn themselves to nightmare, liability to an innocent sister that will eventually marry them, their families and loved ones, even Church and societies Proverbs 22:14.

That reminds me of a friend that was showing interest some year back in Cotonou, God open my eyes to see how big he dresses but with an empty bottle of Star. Some few days later, one of the elders I met told me and said be careful, 'Fawo raja ni o'; meaning he is empty; exactly the insight I received concerning him, that is why as an innocent beloved; you have to hear God before going in Marriage with any man, so that you will not be the one to suffer what other animals have enjoyed. Psalm 11:3 – though the righteous could pray.

It is true when you come to Christ He is able to re-shape your life; pick your pieces and mould you again but, Apa ki ndabi Eran Ara. That is; Scare will forever linger if not permanent. But is far better not to sell our birthright Genesis 25:30-31, Hebrew 12:16-17, 1 Peter 2:19, 3:17, and 4:15.

Another friend was in booming business, he does shuttle between West coast and Nigeria, he was making it then, but unfortunately, he allow Asmodeus to possess him and till today grass are the occupant of his place of business; his own is even terrible he sleep with girls in his office, a place of business; I do not know if he has changed the last bathroom slippers I saw him with last Proverbs 2:16-19, 7: 1-end but; I suggest you concentrate on verses 26-27.

I love sharing this particular testimony. In 2002 I went on for Prayer at one Mountain in Osun State, those of us that are familiar with this Mountain will know of a truth that Jehovah Elohim is a Great Rock;

ninety-nine steps of rocks and my first time of going there, when I finish climbing I busted to tear in fact I had compassion on myself and I even went there on the nightfall. Back then on Friday Night of Prayers, there was a man brought out by the Spirit and he was asked the number of Molue (this Lagos big buses) he has and he answered Six (6) and four tippers with three building and again he was asked what happen to them, he said he has sold them all except the face me and face you apartment the committee of friend did not allow him to sell and it was one of his good friend that knows him too well that brought him for prayer for the first time on that mountain, all these befell him because one of his concubines he sleeps with who was a strange woman and all these happen to him just because this adulterous woman asked for 20,000 nairas and did not quickly give her Proverb 20:17, 30:20, Proverbs 22:14.

The demon of Asmodeus not only using the females in these ways, in fact, the new way of his and her operation now is to look for a clean sister both inside church and outside church to destroy; either to renew the riches, power, fame and affluence he gave his followers because he know that once the hedge of protection of a sister is broken because of sin; OYO – (On your Own) for that sister he know that the sister will not able to fights back John 9:31, unlike their other counterpart in the world that will always move about with another counteract powers in form of rings, powder or makeup and or waist beads Matthew 12:25-26.

Please, beloved and cherished ones in Christ shine your eyes, do not allow any unscrupulous man use you and dump you for another innocent sister somewhere else; anyone wants to sleep with you should go for a proper wedding procedures in the presence of God and man with many witnesses. Proverb 5:16, Song of Solomon 4:12.

The demon Asmodeus work together with Ashtoreth the other principality, Apollo or Abaddon of which queen of heaven is their representative, this queen of heaven love White colour and enjoy rice for sacrifice, she favour her follower and answered their request in affluence, in the book of Prophet Jeremiah had a record about her "Then all the men who knew that their wives were burning incense to other gods, along with all the women who were present—a large assembly—and all the people living in Lower and Upper Egypt, said to Jeremiah, "We will not listen to the message you have spoken to us in the name of the LORD! We will certainly do everything we said we would: We will burn incense to the Queen of Heaven and will pour out drink offerings to her just as we and our fathers, our kings and our officials did in the towns of Judah and in the streets of Jerusalem. At that time we had plenty of food and were well off and suffered no harm. But ever since we stopped burning incense to the Queen of Heaven and pouring out drink offerings to her, we have had nothing and have been perishing by sword and famine." Jeremiah 44:15-18, 7:18.

In 1992, I remember one of the insights I received where I was pleading with some Minister of God to leave her; back then I saw her in the revelation she was portrayed as a flowing Sea, but not as big as a Sea and those men told me No; they cannot leave her because she gives to them Bag of Rice every year. I insisted and told them Christ and Apostles have a better Bag of rice and then they agreed to follow me and we all entered into a sailing boat on the peaceful clean flowing river and I woke up. Asmodeus is not easy to tackle with and he should not be allowed to negotiates with us, in fact, Bible admonishes us to flee from her 1Thessanolians 5:22-23. Revelation 2:20.

Beelzebub is the demon of flies; he is in charge of all kind of ailments and sickness that responds not to treatment, he sucks blood and transfer disease through blood, the demon or spirit of Ogaeso work under him to sucked pregnancies, removes children from women's womb and supplies them to the marine world.

Mammon is in charge of money ritual and source of evil money. This demon work indirectly or directly with the Asmodeus and demon called djoko and djakata they inflict their victim with serious poverty and acute frustration that lead to arm robbery he is greed and un-contentment demon; that is why you see love of money is the cause for prostitution and arm robbery they walk hand in hands 1Timothy 6:9-10, Proverbs 15:27, 23:4, 28:20.

Paimon: is in charge of false prophets, vision, and false tongue and prophesy, he has demon of Cyriel and Orion working for him, they possess power to steal into spiritual realm through evil networking or links, they see for their victims through objects such as mirror, magic board/cards, water basin or pots and their palms Deuteronomy 18:9-14.

I remember in one of the insight Spirit of God gave to me when He was unfolding Deeper on the Issue of Women Revelation that I discussed in chapters that follow, I saw it that a young lady was prophesying with her head not cover with head tie or veil and she had a mirror sized of her palm; she prophesy out of that mirror stacked to her palms; as I notice this I shouted on her to keep quiet, she did not answer and I then said in the Name of Jesus Christ keep quiet, then she left church with almost everyone in the church including a man with short knickers and top that stood in the revelation as a pastor.

Ariton is in charge of inflicting agonies, pain, tortures and destruction on Man, he steal, kill and destroy by magical means such as dolly pinched with needles or magic mirror, and more also this demon fast for revenge Roman 12:19, Leviticus 19:18, 2 Thessalonians 1:5-7 (see one of the true testimonies mention above) Isaiah 58:4, they are the source of any unpleasant situation and anything that are not good, they are the source of sickness and problem that cannot be explained and or; get solutions.

If we do not recognize the differences between divine Angels and these demons, how should we combats with them, some of them are revealed by their names and activities Genesis 44:15-19, Judges 2:11-13, Leviticus 20:2.

The body of Christ needs to publicly and privately, constantly and always resist the devil and all his emissaries of destructions.

We need to rebuke them sharply in Word and in our Prayers every day we gather in the church; in our life and that of our loved ones. Either we know them by name or activities; we shall continually resist them in the Names of our Lord Jesus Christ, by His divine blood, divine Godhead Living Word and Testimonies James 4:7. Revelation 12:11, and John 16:33.

When Jesus was in agony in the garden of Gethsemane, an angel was sent to strengthen Him, Luke 22:43. We may trust in the same way of help from God in our day of trouble and agony, Ps.46:1, but we are not always aware of this, for those who are not in harmony with God's will; an angel may be sent to destroy that person, read Acts 12:23.

Let's thank God for the ministry of His angels and be found on God's side in order to experience the blessings of His divine Angels.

THE TWO REALMS

SPIRITUAL AND PHYSICAL

The spiritual realm is a realm where all spirits relate. It so real and does not pretend to speak lies except when manipulated or misinterpreted. Spiritual realms are with Laws of which if individual understands it; is to his or her own advantage of successful living on the earth planet, that was the reason, the Gift of discerning spirits is highly compulsory and important in this Dark Age we are in.

The spiritual world may entail a guide to directions, the decision to take, restitution to make; a wrong to right and even someone to avoid.

God has never ceased from meeting his creatures in the spirit realm. If God open your spiritual eye or guide you along to understand spiritual realm, it will surely be of great privilege as such; and it will give you a focus and directions in life but if you make mistakes or disobey God's schooling and leading in life through the realm of the spirit, there bound to be disasters, destruction of destiny and your sailing boat in life will be slow. Jonah 1; 1-17. You better understand spiritual realm activities and stay at the centre of God's divine will for your life. Look at the world as created by God, It sees a spiritual realm beyond the five senses.

Each of these realms sees God from different perspectives. Each of them results in different behaviour driven on these physical Worlds. This is the reason why only individuals cannot adequately explain; who we are, where we came from, and why we act the way we do. How you viewed the worlds in which we live, it has a great impact on your understanding and gives a response to the way we experience the spiritual realm.

The realm of the spirits is very real; though we cannot perceive it with our natural senses, only by the gifts of Discerning of Spirit. This gift gives the ability to see supernaturally into the spirit realms as divine God's Spirit wills. If one was informed about a spirit and does not have a vision of the spirit, he or she cannot discern it, by the gift of discerning of the Spirit we see beyond the sphere for which we have been created.

The Occult, Witches and Diviners only steal into Spiritual realms through an objects; such as Mirror, Ouijas boards, Water Pots or third eye etc., and also through the knowledge of good and evil gained in the Garden of Eden 1 Samuel 28:4:15, Acts16:16-19, Deuteronomy 18:9-14.

In the spiritual world, not every transaction carried out can be allow staying in our physical life, we claiming the good ones and quickly reject the opposite on the awakening with prayers. The reason is this; God Almighty created Man in three Parts – Spirit, Soul, and body. We all know that body is what makes differences to live on earth and if any spirits want to stay on earth it must get a body in other to adapt to operation on earth. All the activity carries on in the spiritual realms are the same as on physical earth.

A sister would have been deceiving away from Christ and had been she did not cry for Christ help in that spiritual state, that is how she could have to join evil spiritual merchandise at the expense of her soul and she might even see pretending attending church and going to all necessary services and fellowship with the brethren because she asked for help from a wrong person of a wrong source.

Dear friends, you see; it is not always advisable to ask someone to show you exactly the route he or she take to make it in life, instead report every unpleasant situation you are facing to God your Creator, He alone knows what to do, He know exactly who He will send to help you. The Spiritual realm was so real that some will be eating inside it and whatever they are eating will be the same food on their mouth on awakening or vomits likewise in the physical world. What make man different from Spirit; is the body: when human sleep; it leave us with our spirit and soul alive and alert to function. Isaiah 26:9, 2Corinthians 12:2, Psalm 63:6, 77:2.

God created human beings to experience life -- with the mind, emotion, will, body, and spirit (soul or spirit or inner being depending on your interpretation of New Testament references to soul and spirit). Our "Physical" is partly our assessment of reality through our five senses - sight, smell, taste, hear, and feel. Through our inner being, we digest and analyse the sensory facts. Then, we react to the world around us. Experiences become further facts that shape our understanding and opinion of the Physical world. Our physical also includes our reaction to spiritual influences.

I remembered one of my elder in the Faith during the guide sections at the Church premises we were discussing about the power of insights and Baba told us his testimony about a woman from his village that was tied down in his insights with a strong thick rope and about 2:00pm one day in the afternoon he went to the tree the woman was tied and he loose the woman and pray for her and when he inquire about the woman physically he was told that the woman was seriously on unexplainable sickness for many months but about 2:00pm of exact time baba saw her in his dream the woman was completely healed, she was able to get up from that infirmity and

35

went about free – The same woman, the same place that particular tree was – was the same place the compound of the woman, the same hour baba dreamt was exactly the same hour she was delivered as it was Spiritually so it was Physically

God gives the light of creation, conscience, and Christ to every human being. How we respond to the light given by God determines the non-sensory part of our world view. The worldview then becomes the basis or standard against which we analyse and react to all sensory and spiritual facts. What we believe largely drives our behaviour in light of the facts we receive. Emotions and physical conditions can certainly play a part in our behaviour. But, in the long run, beliefs and genuine Spiritual phenomenon win out. So what we believe about the world around us and what lies beyond the five senses plays a critical role in how we live.

For example; those that believe that life evolves from elemental substance will then believe that there is no God and they are not accountable to Him. They may live a completely unprincipled existence simply to please themselves; lying to gain favors or sympathy murdering anyone so called enemy or whatsoever stand on their way to evil, especially, when they know that they can get away with it Proverb 6:16-19. For some who traverse down this path, they do whatever pleases them even if they know that they will surely get caught. The long-term effects of this physical worldview can be devastating to individuals and societies that leave Divine God out of their Spiritual states and consequently their physical world.

If I believe the Bible; (of that I owe my entire life), then I must submit to God who authored it. He alone has the right to determine right and wrong for my life. All of my life, all sensory and spiritual input, will be subjected to the Authority of God's word and His divine Principles. What is right and true will be kept. What contradicts, compromises, or confuses the truth revealed by God in His word must be rejected. Thus, a biblical perceptive has a dramatic impact on my perception and reaction to reality.

The two major sets of people that see into realms of Spirit are the Seers and the Prophets and also, individual born again child of God can receive Word from their Creator and or have an opportunity to glance into the realm of Spirit for their individual leading and direction from God through dreams. For examples Joseph, Solomon, Nebuchadnezzar, they were not mentioned as a prophet in the scripture, yet they had a dream and spiritual realm experiences for their existences.

'All seers are prophets but not all prophets are seers.' The main difference between a prophetic Seer and a Prophet is the avenue in which they receive revelation. A prophet can be a non-seeing prophet or a seer. 1 Chronicle 29:29.

A seer is one whose prophetic ministry is largely based in the realm of receiving from the Lord in the form of dreams and visions. Seers have a larger percentage of their prophetic gift centred on vision, receiving messages, and revelation knowledge by dreams and visions. In another hand the Seer is with Authoritative Revelatory prophesy 1 Corinthians 14:30

A non-seeing prophet receives auditory revelation either through spoken communication in their spirit or through a message delivered to their spirit. The difference between a spoken message to their spirit and words delivered to their spirit is that sometimes the Words come from God verbatim and other times God just drops an entire message into our spirit, like a package, which we then have to articulate and communicate through the English language.

In other words, this kind of Prophet are those were asked to judge by other prophets because they operate in what I can term as Phenomenon Prophesy 1 Corinthians 14:29

A Seer's main source of revelation comes through vision. They will receive revelation in the form of vision, through pictures, images, and sometimes colours and shapes. Along with the visual revelation, they sometimes get a divine understanding or interpretation, and/ or emotions and feeling by revelation. However, seers do not always understand what they are seeing. Daniel and John did not understand much of what they saw. They simply documented what they saw faithfully. Number 12:6, Hosea 12:10, Acts 2:17

A seer sees things related to their area of anointing and ministry. God does not give divine revelation in a void or for our entertainments. If He is giving the revelation it is for a purpose. The difference between a prophet's dreams and those of another person is that a prophet will receive messages for the future and for the body of Christ. An individual who is not prophetic will usually dream of things that God is speaking to them regarding themselves.

'The main purpose for those with a dream and vision anointing is to awaken the people of God to the spirit realm. It is a miraculous manifestation of the Spirit that creatively illuminates truth and can confirm the direction of God that has been given to others a good biblical example is Prophet Zechariah and more also; one of the true purposes of this great privileges of the Spirit is to have passion to evangelize Christians, non-Christians and the general World alike with the messages that; God is speaking today through dreams and visions in the Realms of Spirits

Personal Testimonies about the Realms

In 1988 I was in the spirit one night and there was a young girl I was trying to lay hand on for deliverance from marine spirit, as I was praying for her deliverance my right thigh began to swollen, I quickly notice this and even by the time I notice my thigh almost get busted and immediately in that revelation I quickly commanded that everything should go back to her and immediately my thigh came back to normal and I woke up.

In 1994 the revelation comes live, exactly the girl, her clothes, and her dressing as in the insight of 1988 was the same, as one of the ushers within deliverance and prayer team brought her to me for prayer, Holy Spirit instantly just brought to my mind the insight of 1988, the next thing I did was that I just walked away from her. The sister usher that brought her was my friend and this angered her and it was like I am getting proud is it because I pray for people and they fall under anointing? I just let her know that it was not so and she will not understand. Even that very day Divine Spirit of God reminds me of another set of vision; the vision of a yam; not knowing that that very day I will be call upon by the elders to join the deliverance team to minister at down basement of Sanctuary because of women candidates for deliverance. The very morning of that day I was picking a big round cut yam inside the sac and I got to a point whereby a hard short strong head of yam from nowhere jumped on top of big yam I was picking, and instantly; I picked the hard small yam and fling it away and I discovered that some were peeping watching what will become of me and I woke up.

Dear friend you can see here that as it was in the spirit realm so was it in physical, even with that kind of six years differences there was no difference between what I saw back then in1988 and what came up 1994.

In the beginning of this chapter I made it clear that Spiritual realm does not lie, except for human manipulation, misinterpretation or we did not see to it at all Jeremiah 14:14, 23:16, Ezekiel 13:3/6. Meanwhile, not all we are privileged to see spiritually; should we communicate openly, sometimes this could be for individual digestion; and or for public or general messages it all depends on divine instruction that follows. Before you say anything about anyone, ask yourself, "Do I have all the facts and physical evidence?" because the information

Holy Spirit gives to us at time is for individual only either as a knowledge or to intercede in prayers, God commands you to "Prove all things; hold fast that which is good" I Thess. 5:21, Micah 7:5, Lev. 19:16-18, Prov. 6:16-19; The sharing of Spiritual messages should base on when we are very sure that sovereign Spirit of God want us to share it or there is an urgency because it involves loss of life or massive damage to the body of Christ Mattew 10:27-28. The Realm of the Spirits is real.

Another insight I had was in 1998 when I was on a visit to my friend place in Abeokuta. When I got to the house I did not meet her, so I decided to go to church, on my way at the roundabout of Oke Ata at about 11:00am my eyes was open to see a girl of about 10/11years crying and pleading to a pregnant woman to allow her to enter her, the woman shouted on her 'get behind me in Jesus name, then I came back to see physical again. On Sunday that same woman came out to share the testimony; not even knowing that the woman was a member of my friend church. You see; that's why this Wednesday's pregnant mothers and expectant mother's prayer meetings are very important.

THE CHURCH AND ADMINISTRATION

*WHEN WE ARE GIVEN AN ASSIGNMENT IN THE
CHURCH AND OR CONCERNING THE BODY OF
CHRIST WE ARE OFTEN GIVEN THE RESPONSIBILITY
TO ALSO DETERMINE HOW TO ACCOMPLISH
THAT ASSIGNMENT. SOMETIMES, HOWEVER, WE
ARE ASKED TO FULFIL AN ASSIGNMENT WITH
SPECIFIC INSTRUCTIONS - HOW IMPORTANT
IS IT TO FOLLOW THOSE INSTRUCTIONS?*

*EZEKIEL 43:10-11, 44:5, DEUTERONOMY 12:32, 32:46,
REVELATION 22:18*

MAN

Man (Anthropos) is created and sustained by God. Gen. 1:27 Acts 17:25, 28. The man is a person and is, therefore, capable of making moral choices. The man is made in the image of God. Gen. 1:27 the image of God is the key to man's identity. The man is God's representative. Gen. 9:6 Man is a picture of God in some respects. Gen.1:26-31. Men ought to Love the Lord their God with all their heart and with all their soul and with their entire mind and with all their strength. The second is this: to Love their neighbour as themselves. God is always; and shall be with Man until eternity John 15:3-12, Roman 12:6-13.

In Psalm 8:4 (read all quoted scripture passages) we find the question what is the man that Thou art mindful of him? Or in a modern translation: What is the man that you remember him? Or what is the man that you think about him? Yes, it is good to know that we are on God's mind and that He remembers us; we are the product of His creation so He has an investment and interest in us. The three basic truth of life was: we came from God who made/created us; we are here to give glory to God, obey Him and worship Him for what He has done for us. And it is our destiny, to live forever and ever, with Him and not to die.

In the book of Genesis chapter 2, we can see all fundamental aspect of Man (Aner); God created man with the purpose to serve Him and praise Him, and as a God Servant, he was placed in the Garden of Eden to take care of it; and man received his first assignment to carry out God's commandments Gen 2:16. Man name all creatures on earth and those names remain till date Gen. 2:19. Man is strong in nature; he is powerful and responsible to be a promise Keeper, he is commanded to honour Jesus Christ through worship, prayer, bring tithes/offering and good substances to the house of God and also obedience to God's Word in the power of the Holy Spirit, 1Timothy 2:8.

Man will rule with Christ and judge all angels 1 Cor. 6:3. He is commanded to repent and make restitutions where necessary, he is to pursue vital relationships to practise spiritual, moral, ethical, and sexual purity and also to build strong marriages and families through love, protection, and biblical values, the man God's mission on earth was to His church by honouring and praying for his brethren, and by actively giving his time and resources to reaching beyond any racial and denominational barriers to demonstrate the power of biblical unity and to influencing his world, being obedient to the Great Commandment Mark 12:30-3 and the Great Commission Matthew 28:19-20.

In these entire positive commandment given to man yet he has another command of "Do Not". 1Cor. 11:7 - A man ought not to cover his head since he is the image and glory of God, but the woman is the glory of man. A man ought not to kill for any reason or serve other gods. He is not to bear false witness or cause discord Proverb 6:16-19. A man shall Not Multiply Wives:

"Deuteronomy 17:17 says that you should not multiple wives, which is a direct command not to be polygamous!"

"But he shall not multiply horses to himself, nor cause the people to return to Egypt (that is he should not become a tyrant or taskmaster, he should not be bully in nature), to the end that he should multiply horses: forasmuch as the LORD hath said unto you, ye shall henceforth return no more that way. Neither shall he multiply (Hebrew 'Rabah') wives to himself that his heart turns not away: neither shall he greatly multiply to himself silver and gold." Deuteronomy 17:16-17, that a man should live moderately and not too extravagancy Hebrew 12:1-2, 12-16, Psalm 62:10, Matthew 6:19, 1Timothy 6:9-10, 3:3, Colossians 3:5.

"Of the nations concerning which the LORD said unto the children of Israel, Ye shall not go into them, neither shall they come in unto you: for surely they will turn away your heart after their gods: Deut. 22:5. Solomon clave unto these in love and he had seven hundred wives, princesses, and three hundred concubines: and his wives turned away his heart. For it came to pass, when Solomon was old, that his wives turned away his heart after other gods: and his heart was not perfect with the LORD his God, as was the heart of David his father." 1 Kings 11:2-4 say "Shall we then hearken unto you to do this entire great evil, to transgress against our God in marrying strange wives?" Nehemiah 13:27 "Give not thy strength unto women, nor thy ways to that which destroyed kings." Proverbs 2:19, 5:1-7, 22:14, 31:3.

For those of us that know Biology, we know that a man is the only sex that gives identity to a child since the woman only has to release an X chromosome because that all she could provide and the man has both X and Y chromosomes to release. If a man releases X chromosome the child will be a girl and if he releases Y the child will be a boy, we can see that in this simple science fact, God in His infinite wisdom had designed a man different from woman, that is why a man are with more blood and stronger than a woman.

There are differences between being a boy and a man, there was a saying that 'to be a man is not a day job, you did not measure a man by sizes, for the fact that you build some muscles or a successful businessman does not make you a man, a man his a divine representative of God; having moral and godly qualities, ability in self-control, able to stand in the gap for both his Home, church, and Societies.

The eternal and original designs pattern of God is for a man to be His ambassador on Earth, and to stand in the gap of Leadership and Authority to take good care of both their wives, children, families, church and societies Genesis 2:15-19, 1Timothy 3:1-13, Luke 2: If you go through the entire bible on your own you will discover all about what man ought to be; do and not to do Deut. 12;28 and besides; not all men have the Spirit of God.

In conclusion, Man is wonderfully made and created, God is highly proud of the man, yet; He will bring man into judgment at the end of this entire world. Ecclesiastes 11:9, 12:14, Psalm 98:9, Matt 16:27, Roman 2:6, Revelation 20:12.

Personal Experience:

I remember in one of the night; I did not sleep deep, it is like a thought in my subconscious or information drop into my spirit man and He was telling me this 'Do you know that any unpleasant situation I allow to come to men is like 10%, the one I allow Satan was like 20% but remaining 70% are from Man. I was surprised and I could not place it properly for some time until when I began to grow more in understanding. And also I remember that I read or a sister said the same things as a confirmation Genesis 22:1, James 1:13-14. When you read through entire stories in the Bible, especially a book such as Psalms 140 – 144 you will discover what man can do to his fellow man only God can deliver him out of such.

WOMAN

The birth of Christ, His divine teaching and Christianity have release Women from virtual bondage, extricate her from the base position of a Man's holding, or property and set her at liberty in the most exalted place in the system of social ethics the world has ever known. Under the Judaism her position was very much higher and honoured as a mother; respect was paid to her. She was not an article of personal property that is why bride price will be paid to her from her husband to her father. She was only allowed to issue divorce bill when indecency was found in her but whatsoever we categorised indecency in our today's world Christ had come to set her free through His death and blood shed on Calvary. Meanwhile, in Paganism, they were abused as the weaker vessels and maltreated like a slave, men stood superior over women they even proclaimed and thank God for not creating them as a woman and they can even be removed into the bed chamber and beaten there. In so many places in the world and even today generation, women were reduced to unconditional and lowered often to shameful status and conditions. The men made them carry heavy loads like a camel beast and indulge them in all sort of drudgery and being a weaker vessel she was always exploited and became a plaything and a slave.

Women are precious unto God Jehovah and He sent His divine son Jesus Christ to die for them also, Galatians 3:26-28. She was also called by inspiration; the co-heir, fellow-participant of the grace of Life 1Peter 3:7.

Yet; we must face the truth that a woman is not a man, God has not given unto woman a place of Leadership and Authority.

A Christian and divinely obedient woman have her own divinely appointed role, sphere and places in which God intended her to serve, and into which a man intrudes only when he is a fool. A man has an assignment and station also appointed by God into which it is folly for a woman to intrude and God will see her as disobedient and a witch. 1Samuel 15:22-23, Proverb 21:3, Eccl.5:1, Jeremiah 7:23. The place of a woman is not less honourable or less influential than that of a man Luke 10:39-42.

WOMEN IN DRESSING

What is the Bible's view on the woman's dressing and her places in the body of Christ and her home? And or, are all these rules about her roles and duties naturally assigned to her would be part of her criteria to heaven? Many people wonder what advice the Bible gives on these questions 1John 2:17, Luke 17:27.

I will like to recall the purpose of this chapter in this book that we are making plain what ought to be in the kingdom of divine Godhead with His Principles and Pattern. And not a malicious ideal – In another word the total function and administration of divine spirituality is not and can never be the same with that of secular world John 17:16

Does the Bible have a dress code for Women? 'YES. The clothing worn in Biblical times was very different from what we wear today both men and women wore a loose, woollen, robe-like cloak or mantle as an outer garment. It was fastened at the waist with a belt or sash. A tunic or coat, a long piece of cloth, leather or haircloth with holes for arms and head, was worn under the cloak. Sandals were worn on the feet. The difference between men's and women's clothing was small but distinctive. In addition, men often wore a turban to confine their hair, and women of some cultures wore a veil.

Now one of the controversial issues was, should women wear Trousers to church? In the book of Deuteronomy, the Word of God prohibit against dressing in clothing of the opposite sex? A woman must not wear men's clothing, or a man wears women's clothing for the LORD your God detests anyone who does this. Deuteronomy 22:5

No one knows for sure whether this prohibition was intended as a general principle or was directed at some specific abuse among the ancient Hebrews. But, I believe it of the generic rule because God declares His mind here; and centred it on the pattern for Worship instead of secular life. Cross-dressing was likely considered an affront to the natural distinction between the sexes Genesis1:27. It may also have been related to some deviant sexual practice, Roman 1:26-27, or more likely, to pagan worship.

One scholar's Commentator; Matthew Henry; makes some worthwhile comments on Deuteronomy 22:5. He wrote thus: " ... Some think it refers to the idolatrous custom of the Gentiles: in the worship of Venus, women appeared in armours, and men in women's clothes; this, as other superstitious usages, is here said to be an abomination to the Lord ... It forbids the confounding of the dispositions and affairs of the sexes: men must not be effeminate and a woman been virago ... " It is known that some pagan rituals of that time involved women wearing armour and men dressing as women, and the Hebrews were forbidden to do anything that had even the appearance of pagan worship 2 John 1:10.

Some people think this verse would prohibit women from wearing trouser because it has traditionally been worn by men. But, in light of the similarity of men's and women's clothing in Biblical times and the fact that trouser was not worn by either sex at that time, that conclusion would be difficult to justify.

Meanwhile, with the understanding of this context in Matthew Henry Commentary Bible, I believe it is wrong for a woman to come to the congregations of Saints on Trousers or with any clothing appear to be used by men. Pantaloons or Trouser could be worn in secular world or outside church, but when we are coming to worship as a body of Christ or gathering to appear before God Almighty as to worship, we have to lay to our heart His divine Principles and Pattern in our worship to Him and we have to change our clothing/garments in other to conform to that appearance suitable for each sex before God Jehovah Genesis 35:2, 1Corinthians 11:1-10, 1Timothy 2:9-11

Whichever, contextual or remote contextual restriction placed on the general teaching of Deuteronomy 22:5. The same principle is seen in the New Testament. Paul wrote: "Doth not even nature itself teach you, that, if a man has long hair, it is a shame unto him?" (1 Cor. 11: 14). A Clear distinction is made between the domestic roles of men and women Eph. 5: 22 Sharp differentiations are also seen between the function of men and women in religious matters. For instance, men are to be the leaders in the public worship of God (I Tim. 2: 8-15). Also, men are to be the elders and preachers of God's people (1 Tim. 3: 1-7; Tit. 1: 5-11, 1 Tim. 2: 12-15). The movement, to make a gender-free society; is in opposition to the plain teaching of God's word.

MIXED MATERIALS: - There was also a prohibition against wearing clothes woven of wool and linen together: Do not wear clothes of wool and linen woven together. Deuteronomy 22:11, again, no one is sure why this would be wrong. It may have been to avoid mixing things that God has created separately Deuteronomy 22:9-11, Leviticus 19:19 or, these mixtures may have been related to some idolatrous practice that the Hebrew was forbidden to imitate Deuteronomy 22:5. There are two passages in the New Testament concern proper dress for women:

I also want women to dress modestly, with decency and propriety, not with braided hair or gold or pearls or expensive clothes, but with good deeds, appropriate for women who profess to worship God. 1 Timothy 2:9-10

Paul is not the only New Testament writer who addressed the Christian's women style of dressing. Peter, through the same guidance of the Holy Spirit, wrote that Christian women "adorning let it not be that outward adorning of plaiting the hair, and of wearing of gold, or putting on of unnecessary extravagant apparel: But let it be the hidden man of the heart, in another word, a woman beauty should not come from outward adornment, it should be that of inner self, the unfading beauty of a gentle and quiet spirit, which is of great worth in God's sight. For this is the way the holy women of the past who put their hope in God used to make themselves beautiful. (1 Peter 3:2-5)

Many of the New Testament letters address specific abuses that occurred in the early Christian communities, and that may be the case here. Jesus had defied the standards of first-century male-dominated society by treating women as equals. Paul had declared all people equal in the family of God Galatians 3:26-29. Many Bible scholars believe some women in the church had carried their "liberation" too far and adopted offensive styles of dressing. Church leaders were anxious to avoid any hint of scandal in the churches, and these passages served that purpose. Both of these passages also make the point that a person's true beauty comes from within and is properly expressed by good deeds rather than showy clothing and jewellery.

A few Christians interpret these passages as a requiring woman to dress very plainly and refrain from wearing jewellery or using makeup. But most Christians believe this advice is simply to dress modestly and in good taste, according to the standards of the society they live in that which did not oppose divine rule in the Word of God.

Should women have a head covering or veil to church: - Apostle Paul address proper head covering for worship in his letters to the church at Corinth, Paul responded to a number of questions the Corinthian Christians had asked him 1 Corinthians 7:1. One of those questions involved proper head covering during worship services. No one knows what the exact question was or what situation prompted it, but Paul gave this reply:

Any man who prays or prophesies with something on his head disgraces his head, but any woman who prays or prophesies with her head unveiled disgraces her head–(both Godhead and her husband) –it is one and the same thing as having her head shaved. For if a woman will not veil herself, then she should cut off her hair; but if it is disgraceful for a woman to have her hair cut off or to be shaved, she should wear a veil. For a man ought not to have his head veiled, since he is the image and reflection of God; but the woman is the reflection of the man. (NRSV, 1 Corinthians 11:4-7)

In first century culture, it was considered a mark of respect for a man to remove his turban in the presence of a superior. Similarly, a man should remove his head covering when he came into God's presence in prayer. Additionally, it was the custom of pagan men to cover themselves while praying, so as to avoid distractions. Thus, men who profess the true Godhead should remove their head coverings to avoid any association with paganism.

Jewish women did not normally wear veils, but reputable Greek and Roman women did. A woman's veil was a symbol of her modesty and respect for her husband. For a Corinthian woman to remove her veil in public would have been an insult to her husband and an affront to the Greek/Roman society in which she lived. Paul strongly discouraged any such rebellion or hint of scandal within the churches. In addition, some pagan priestesses removed their veils and wore their hair dishevelled when prophesying. Thus, women should remain veiled while praying or prophesying to avoid any association with paganism. (See the example I gave above under Angel about a lady prophesying with a mirror in her palm)

It must have been a great disgrace for a woman to shave her head. So, Paul made the comparison that removing one's veil while praying or prophesying would be an equally great disgrace.

The Bible's rules about dress cannot be misunderstood or look down upon, yet, the general principles of modesty and propriety can be applied. We should dress for public worship in a way that is generally considered appropriate. Standards of dress change over time and are different from church to church, but we should avoid any style of dress that is offensive or sends a message opposing the church community's values.

Whenever we look at the Word of God, let us keep the principles in mind and not violate or avoid the intent of its teachings. Improper dress should not be a problem for the Christians, and if it is, the person should do some soul searching. The person who has repented, being born again and having taken up his cross to follow Christ and commandment of God Almighty should lovingly and joyfully followed His Divine Word. And also, we should remember 'Is Because Of Angels' 1Corinthians 11:9-10.

WOMEN IN WORSHIP

Why is there so much confusion in churches over this subject? "For God is not the author of confusion, but of peace, as in all churches of the saints." – I Corinthians 14:33. Some will say that it was their tradition and doctrine of their founder or pioneered of a vision to appoint women as a reverend, pastors etc. of churches. But, that is not the truth! What I think or feel about any subject or Christian issues is really not that important, but what God's Word has to say is the final authority on any and all subjects and issues concerning Bodies of Christ. I have heard one of the Papa of Faith in this Generation that said God asked him who is the reverend between Him and himself, he was surprised at the question and finally answered God that you are the Reverend and since that awakening he decided to be called a Pastor, therefore if God can correct one of His beloved servants in this manner where did we get a false impression and wrong title of calling woman a reverend or giving a title God does not recognize which they were given. 1Sam.15:23

God in His infinite mercy had drawn me to Himself for almost forty years, the Almighty God Is true to His Word- Jesus Christ Is the truth, and Holy Spirit Is true. The Godhead will NEVER contradict Himself on anything. The Holy Spirit will NEVER lead anyone to do anything that contradicts the Bible which is God's Word. So, open your Bibles and see what the Bible has to say concerning your claim dreams and impulsiveness that was claimed to be the leading of God's Spirit. We are reading and hearing so much today about the confusion among churches and associations because of many wrong issues in the body of Christ.

One of the most devastating, and debilitating, and destructive movements in our day is the "Feminist Movement." - It is changing not only the world but sadly it is changing the church, and as a result, the Word of God is being dishonoured; opponents are having many things to say about us and God our Saviour is being dishonoured and shamed. Radical feminism has brainwashed our culture, it has brainwashed our culture to the degree that even the church has fallen victim to this, church Leaders, Theologians, Professors of theology who are supposed to be profound in the Scripture, as well as lay people in the church have bought the feminist lies.

A church will call a woman preacher, or she will take Spiritual Leadership roles in churches. This should not be a matter of confusion. Since every church is autonomous (independent), and can do as they desire; therefore, a church should be SURE that what they practise is in accordance with the Word of God. God is not the author of confusion if every church stuck to the Bible we would not have the confusion we have today concerning this issue and much other more. He created man and quite some time later extracted woman out of the man, in essence, the Word says that man and woman have equal access to salvation through Christ (Gal 3:28) BUT the purpose of man and his functions are clearly different from that of a woman. Most Everyone That Is In Heresy On This Subject Quotes This Verse Of Scripture - "There is neither Jew nor Greek, there is neither bond nor free, there is neither male nor female, for ye are all one in Christ." - Galatians 3:28 - This particular place was just simply on Salvation that belongs to every Man on Earth. He is not dealing With the Matter of the Place of Service, but with Salvation; that is, they were all saved by the same grace of God.

Jesus Faced The same Problem in His Day with Religious Leaders; going by the Tradition of Men instead of by The Word of God Matthew 15:3-6, the Bible is clear on this matter. It is not what tradition says, it is not what the popularity of the day says, it is not what certain groups believe, NO, it is what the Word Of God says that stand; Teachers that is what important. Act 4:19, 5:29, Daniel 3:16-18. In another hand, we have to understand that Secularism and Traditions are not the same functions as divine Spirituality; is just like the way a King's anointing is distinguished from Prophet and Priest with their responsibilities and duties.

The Bible Is Our Perfect Rule Of Faith And Practice. Let all things be done decently and in order" - I Corinthians 14:40. The Lord's church is the pillar and ground of truth in the world, if the church is off; on any subject, the people will not know the truth about the matter. The church usually listens to what the pastor says, but if the pastor is wrong, then the church will usually be wrong. We must keep the church true to the Word of God by teaching the truth on every subject. Compare scripture with scripture just like the Bereans and hold that which is Truth. 1Thess. 5:21, Proverbs. 19:27, Galatians 1:8.

The Jezebel spirit is born of witchcraft and rebellion. This spirit is one of the most common spirits in operation today, both in the church and in the world, and it is a powerful enemy of the body of Christ. She operates freely on sincere believers whose hearts are for God individually and has also attained positions of power as powers and principalities within the Congregation of God (Compare Revelation four below). How could a woman possibly be a pastor when she is forbidden to teach or to have any authority over men? Women can only be pastors if they openly disobey the Bible's teaching.

This spirit establishes its stronghold primarily in women; however, many men have been victimized by it as well, where it functions as a "controlling" spirit. The total purpose of humankind is to bring Glory to God and to glorify His thrice Holy name, forever and ever. The admonition given to us is "whatsoever you do, do all to the glory of God" 1 Corinthians 10:31 this means that ALL we do must have the goal to bring glory to God, anything else is sin and God will not accept it; indeed it brings danger of Hell, and to bring Glory to Him ALL has to be done according to His way Exodus 25:40

WHAT THE BIBLE SAYS CONCERNING THIS ISSUE!

To start with: Joel 2:28 does not support women Ministry in the wrong setting. Let us not escape from reason, please, for if Paul had a split mind, then every single Epistle of his would need to be eradicated from the Bible as unreliable and not inspired by God. This is a God command and divine order (1Corinthian 14:35) and also, this is like a Brimstone of fire or glass ceiling; and Those who would attempt to shatter this ceiling will do so at their own peril and destruction.

I Corinthians 14:34-35; I Timothy 2:11-12 Read your Bible. This is God's Word telling us what God's says about the Woman's place in His church. This is not being popular: or any man-made opinion and ideas! This is God's Word, and we either believe the Word of God or we accept the traditions of man and his opinions (Compare Revelation 3 - 5 below). Acts 4:19, 5:29, Exodus 1:17, Daniel 6:13.

BISHOPS OR PASTORS QUALIFICATION

We know that the Word Bishop can also mean Pastor. The Bible is clear on the qualifications of a pastor. They are to be as Paul says - "A bishop then must be blameless, the husband of one wife." - I Timothy 3:2. There are many qualifications here, but one of them is – not having more than one wife, certainly a woman cannot have a wife as for a husband this is clear and another qualification is - "One that rules well his own house." - I Timothy 3:4. The Bible plainly teaches that the husband is the head of the home. Ephesians 5:22; Colossians 3:18. The husband must know how to rule his own house or he will not be able to take care of the church of God – Ephesians 5:25. There are many other qualifications for a bishop, but certainly, no woman can fill those two qualifications.

THINGS WOMEN SHOULD DO

There are many things that women are permitted to do in the church according to the Bible. Having noticed what women are forbidden to do, let us now notice what they may and should do. They are called Prophetess, missionary along with their husband or in groups, all that pertaining women affairs in the Sanctuary, vestry keeper, Hospitality and Helps, Evangelism (House to House Ministry - Visitations), Holy communion Preparer (Not to shared – this is an Elder's duties) All form of arts and Decorations, Administrators and all other Ministries and duties that is not Anti Godhead in setting or against His divine order Roman 16.

1. They Should Attend Public Worship this is the duty of all saved people. Women should attend public worship to learn and to receive such spiritual blessings as may come from the worship Hebrews 10:25. Every saved soul needs the healing, purifying, and elevating influence of public worship; therefore, women should participate in the Worship by Praying though not on Leadership role 1Tim 2:8.

2. They Should Participate In Congregational Singing. These are also general duties, as well as privileges. Some would say if a woman is not permitted to speak in the church, then she can't sing. But, we must interpret Paul by the intention

manifested in the context, he was not discussing singing, but speaking, and while singing involves speaking; yet, technically, singing is not speaking. Congregational singing is a general duty and privilege, and it belongs to women the same as men.

3. They are to recognize the home as their chief sphere of Activity - Titus 2:5. It is here that a woman is to find her chief work not only in caring for her own family but in entertaining others - I Timothy 5:9, 10. It is here and here alone that she can earn an Angelic and prophet's reward by entertaining prophets and Angels unknowingly Matthew 10:41. Genesis 18: 2-10, 19:1-14, Heb 13:2.

4. The Older Women Are Commanded To Teach the Younger Ones Jeremiah 9:20, Titus 2:3-5. They are specially charged to teach young women practical home duties, but this Scripture does not limit their teaching to this. They are to be - "teachers of good things" verse 3. They are not evangelists; as in the Office or in Leadership and Authority.

In 1989, I had this testimony from one of my Christian Brother, Bother Adebiyi Taiwo. In one of those Saturday of Evangelism and visitation, and I do end my movement in their house because they are my good family friend, his sister was my friend, but not in the Country as at then and she left an aged mother behind of which I took as my responsibility.

There came this blessed day, I went to the house and knock for almost 15minutes, I almost turned back when he came out and open the door and it was like he was just woken up from sleep, and then he was narrating what he saw in the revelation to me; he said in the spiritual realm there was a setting like judgment day and he saw the Lord on His throne, declared judgment on all so called Lady evangelist, the first thing I said was that how could that be, was it that all the Lady Evangelist as at then years back would not make Heaven? And he added that on his awakening they told him to tell me that I will explain better. I did not lay to heart this message until Jehovah himself starts unfolding this issue to me in 1999. (Compare my Personal Experience No. 6 below)

There are many gifted women who might very well do a better job at preaching and teaching than many men. The most Spirit-filled woman, with Revelatory and vocal Gifts of Holy Spirit, might be a tremendous asset to the body of Christ and by grammar or vocabulary we may term or call such a woman; a Prophetess Judge 4:4-7, Mark 16:9-11, John 20:11-18, Acts 21:9. If you study the account of these women and other of their kinds they operates in the call of Godhead in a subordinate setting; Not in the role of Leadership and Authority or in Five Fold Office of Jesus Christ Ephesians 4:10-12. We are to be careful how will trade with the Gifts of God in our life so that will not be dammed at the end. However, it isn't gifting that is the issue, but God's order and calling. The Divine Godhead will never bend His order for any woman or call any woman in contrary to His divine Rule, Principles and Patterns Matthew 7:21-23.

As we have already indicated, the speaking or silence that is forbidden to women is public speaking, or speaking out, in the church assemblies in high platform, travelling up and down leaving her household behind in the name of preaching the gospel or any setting that place her on Leadership and Authority in the gathering of God or Congregation of His people. Praying (that is, leading in prayer) must be included in this Silence. Indeed, 1 Timothy 2:8 specifically states that "men" (in Greek, "males," not "people") are to "pray in every place [of worship], lifting up holy hands [that is, leading in prayer]."

However, it is important to distinguish between an individual addressing the congregation and been in the congregation as a whole worshipping God audibly in the recitation of a prayer or the singing of a hymn. One aspect of such congregational speech is that the members of the congregation speak to one another (Ephesians 5:19), but in this case, no individual teaching or leading is involved, for Example, Special numbers and Testimonies on Salvation; standing within the Congregations with a wireless microphone or on a layman ground.

The Bible teaches that women are not to speak in church, the word speaks used here is a strong verb and not speak as per rapport. This is an apostolic rule that is based on the created order. The fact that our society is in rebellion against the biblical teaching regarding women, does not make the Bible obsolete; it makes us who adopt the world's system and values bring more shameful and dishonouring to the Lord. The similar instruction in 1Timothy 2:11–12 also requires women to remain silent, but more specifically prohibits teaching and other leading. The woman must be careful to remain "in subjection" (that is, not leading the assembly) Roman 2:8.

Remember, whosoever that does not follow the Apostles Doctrines, will follow the doctrines of Demons (Quotes Unknown). Ephesians 2:20, 1Timothy 4:1.

In the complexity of modern church activity, many questions will arise about how to apply Paul's rule of silence. Some may think that it is more important to encourage participation than to abide by a Divine God's given Administrations functions which seem to some people out-of-date rule. Therefore, the question becomes, are we seeking to obey the Word of God or seeking to satisfy ourselves and placate others. I will like to let us know that Subjection is not Inferiority meanwhile that was the divine pattern of God even before the fall. In another word, this is the divine order of Sovereign God.

Note: the Bible ordinarily speaks of wives being subject to their own husbands; Paul here speaks of women, in general, being subject to men in general (obviously in a restricted sense). Men should treat women with special kindness and consideration (compare 1 Timothy

5:1-2), and women should treat men with special respect—at least "in church," but also, according to the situation, wherever the grace of God can bless our relationships.

A Christian bible believing Woman cannot be the head of a Man (Aner) even at home not to talk of a Spiritual gathering of His bodies (Saint) 1Corinthians 11:3, Ephesians 6:1-4. She cannot exercise dominion over Man (Aner) 1Tim 2:12. She cannot lead Public Prayers. 1Tim 2:8. The common word for a man used in the Bible was 'Anthropos' this is generic or a general term for Man and it does state Human being that consist both Males and females. The word Man (Anthropos) were used 516 times in the Bible and the word Man (Aner) used in this very verse of 1Tim 2:8 were used 150 times in the New Testament and not always use. Most times the Man (Aner) used, it was in contrast to the woman and the word phrase 'in Every Place' signified Public gathering of the Bodies (Church) of Christ and all worship in the Tabernacle of the Living God.

She cannot be a public Preacher and Teacher of the word of God in Leadership and Authority Settings. 1 Corinthian.14:34. She cannot be an elder, pastor Reverend or whatsoever; see the set forth requirements as stated in 1Timothy 3:2, Titus 1:6.

In another word, God's giving grace upon woman can expound the Word of God like in the case of Apollo's Act 18:26, 1 Peter 3:1-2. She can pray and prophesy within and inside Congregations of Saint with her head cover with veil, not in a setting that look like her standing above in the Public gathering of Christians assembly if she does she has put herself in Leadership role and Authority of that to God she usurping, disobeying and putting herself in situation divine God does not recognize.

She can guide the home 1Timothy 5:14, she may also school others; like matured ones to school younger women Titus 2:4-5 and she can be a servant in the local church, she can teach and admonish but not interfering the former prohibition. Roman 16:1-2, Ephesians 5:19, Colossians 3:16

God has ordained that only men are to serve in positions of Spiritual Leadership and Authority in the church. This is not because men are necessarily better teachers, or because women are inferior or less intelligent (which is not the case). It is simply the way God designed the church to function. Men are to set the example in spiritual leadership—in their lives and through their words. Women are to take a less authoritative role. Women are encouraged to teach other women Titus 2:3-5.

The Bible also does not restrict women from teaching children. The only activity women are restricted from is teaching men or having spiritual authority over them. This logically would preclude women from serving as pastors/preachers. This does not make women less important, by any means, but rather gives them a ministry focus more in agreement with God's plan and His gifting for them.

Abraham Lincoln once said No man is poor who has a godly mother. Thackeray wrote; Mother is the name for god on the Lips and Heart of Little children and Jewish Talmud asks: who is best taught, then answers: He who first learned from his mother.

Personal Testimonies on this Issue:

In Conclusion concerning these analyses above this is what I received from the Divine Spirit in year 1999/2000.

REVELATIONS ONE:

I found myself kneeling down inside a witness box and I had a voice from heaven which I believe is the voice of God. He told me with all angry countenance, go and tell my servants … … I am angry with them for appointing women into the place of Leadership and Authority. Immediately I got up with the weight of that message, feeling the anger of the Lord, I ran to go forth and relay the message, on my way, I met a deaconess (not married), who I know, she said, even some men do not like it and then I woke up.

REVELATION TWO:

I found myself in a congregation where the minister was preaching, but he is not standing directly at the front, assisted by a deacon who in the front row reading a bible passages for him and to the congregations but, none of them were on the Platform/Altar. I found myself kneeling and suspended in the air at the back of the congregations then, I saw heaven open and a file was dropped into my hand and laps and in that file, I found a white sheet of paper with the diagram below:

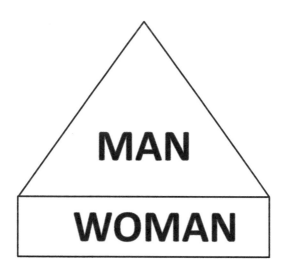

Then, I looked into the open heaven and beheld a picture like a big man with very big hand saying. "Arrange the platform of women low."

REVELATION THREE:

I saw myself in an open field with an unfamiliar brother and a familiar sister who is the head usher at her church. She behaved and talked rudely to the brother, the brother also reacted negatively. I intervened to at least restore peace and corrected the attitude of the sister by telling her that, what she is doing is not scriptural, before I knew what was happening she engaged in serious blow with the brother to the point that other unfamiliar people gathered around them. The brother went ahead to chew off one finger of the sister, immediately, she went on coma and everyone thought she was dead. But on a sudden, she got up with big firewood attempting to hit it on the brother's head but to no success. Afterward, the brother came back to thank me and I woke up.

REVELATION FOUR:

God made me understand that a church with a Prophetic ministry will only allow their women ministrations on the limit. (I studied the bible to know more about the role of women). And I saw a man whom God told me is a true prophet trying to carry out an assignment giving to him by God but I saw a woman rose up against him in the spirit that the assignment will not succeed. This woman was sitting on the Platform/altar with some other men, the prophet got frustrated and I woke up Roman 6:1, 15.

REVELATION FIVE:

I found myself and some women inside a kingdom like that of King Nebuchadnezzar with his golden image around the kingdom, though the king was not on the seat but the chair was there. Then I saw a man beside the image he ordered the women to bow to the golden image at The Shout Of Let Us Worship; all the women bowed down and God told me that they were all bowing to the god of the land. I wanted to go on my knees too, but the story of Daniel chapter 3 just click on my heart in the dream and I resisted that I will not bow and I woke up.

REVELATION SIX:

I found myself stopping some women not to climb the altar/platform, in the process two women I was not familiar with sent me a letter through a lad (boy) but I disregarded the letter and continue telling those women that 'do they think that the altar/platform was just like ordinary blocks or wood"? They were many, and they pushed me aside. Suddenly, I was up the sky sitting. I do not know if I was sitting on a chair or not, I held a jotter and pen writing and I saw all that were going on the Earth, at the same time I saw a basket full of different kinds of fruits jiggled between heaven and earth, the fruits were supposed to come down Roman 6:1, 15. Suddenly, there was problem at centre of the place I was trying to stop those women from climbing the platform/altar, a woman ran to the centre of the place that I was sitting up in the sky and she asked me how many miles to heaven and I answered her 99 million miles, she was disappointed and put her two hands on the head and started crying as if she cannot make it … … …

With all these revelations I strongly believe that God Almighty want His church to really go back to His divine principle and pattern, the holiness in accordance with the standard of the Holy Bible and to the master plan of His worship especially in a public Assembly and the roles of man and woman 1Cor. 14:40, 1 John 2:17, Exodus 27:21. Ezekiel 41:1-10, 42:13-20, 43:6-13, 44:5-24

The Biblical Passages concerning this issue and in accordance to the above revelations are that; I was naturally and basically study the meaning and definition of Leadership and Authority, and Priesthood (verb). The usage of women figuratively and symbolically in the scriptures, I discovered that is not encouraging in relations to what is currently happen in today's world not to talk of allowing them to intrude into the Holy of Holies or Divine things without check And my question is this, does the father has no sons again? Exodus 28:39-43 Leviticus 8:1-13. I believe God use women of old and even in this present generation, the question is this; is the foundation of their ministrations in compliance with the LOGOS (bible) or the RHEMA (spoken) word of God, which are a commandment of God. Lev. 10:1-2, 11 Sam. 6:1-11, Ex. 40:12-38, Matthew 7:21-23, Luke 10:42. I am very sure of this disobedience has nothing to do with God and shall never have a place in God. Matthew 7:21-23, John 10:27, 1John 2:4. And besides, who do will think we are? If devil will not stop at anything but rather contended for the body of Moses we better Watch and Pray 1Peter 4:17. Jude 1:9. Another question is this will they be able to make heaven? Mathew 7: 21-23, 1Corinthians 3:13. And more also; are the wrong setting not hindering the presence of God and His blessing among His people? 1Corinthians 5:6. Compare Revelation 6 above Luke 13:5. I believe Christ has come to make full of God's law Matt. 5:17-18, 1 Cor. 14:40.

For the fact that the women make use more of their two sides brain; compare to a man that concentrates on using one side; does not give us a licence or liberty to array them against the divine principle and pattern of God. The reasons and benefits of both man and woman uses their brain this way was designed by God to complements each other, since the man use one side of the brain; they are more logical, challenge-oriented and direct their thinking pattern and energy in achieving objectives and goals and that is why they are seen as somebody that always on the move, they are fast and focused, while women, are emotional, more sensitive, thinking deeper, has ability to foresight and somehow appear more spiritual, this is a medical fact.

Throughout the scriptures, we read many instances how the blessed Godhead designs His plans and blueprint for entire universe and individuals and even the social research and figures made us understand that when a divine principle and pattern of divine Godhead is maintained, and or; a home where man is a godly father and responsibly committed Christian; have a chance of growing in love and raising a peaceful and committed children, home and societies and the result has to be eternal and strong compare to a place where a woman is an other way round.

It is so obvious that the divine Godhead need a man to stand in the gap and to be in a place of Leadership and Authority both in the homes, churches, and societies 1Timothy 2:8.

Other proved texts: Deut. 22:5, 1 Cor. 11:5-10, 13-14, 1 Cor. 14:34-37, 1 Tim. 2:11-14, Lev. 10:39-42, Exodus 19: 24-25, Exodus 27:21.

YOUTH

Ecclesiastes 12:1

Remember your Creator in the days of your youth, before the days of trouble come and the years approach when you will say, "I find no pleasure in them" Either we believe this or not everyday man woke up to see new day so he or she near his or her grave. And there are no other privileges as for a youth to bear the yokes of Christ early and established himself or herself in Divine Godhead plans and purpose for his or her life Matthew 6:33, John 15:5,16, Lamentation 3:26-27.

Titus2:2-8.

Teach the older men to be temperate, worthy of respect, self-controlled, and sound in faith, in love and in endurance. Likewise, teach the older women to be reverent in the way they live, not to be slanderers or addicted to much wine, but to teach what is good. Then they can train the younger women to love their husbands and children, to be modest and pure, to be busy at home, to be kind, and to be subject to their husbands, so that no one will malign the word of God. Similarly, encourage the young men to be self-controlled. In everything set them an example by doing what is good. In your teaching show integrity, seriousness and soundness of speech that cannot be condemned, so that those who oppose you may be ashamed because they have nothing bad to say about us.

In this passage of the scripture read above, it tells us that the Life of the Youth is far more enriching and important in the hand of God. We need early good training in the home, Church, and societies.

In fact, the development to Elderhood starts from the youthful stage, but there is a need for us to lay our youth foundation properly so that our elderhood life will be so enriched and satisfactory. There is no other way or any other advice I can give to Youth than to read through this book with understanding and fasten themselves with the divine Word of God written down in the Bible and His divine (Rhema) Word that might as well comes to them individually on daily basis from the Divine Holy Spirit of God.

Psalm 119:9 – asked; how can a young man keep his way pure? Then answer; by living according to God's word. Psalm 119:105 God's word is a lamp to my feet and a light for my path.

The Almighty God our creator from the beginning had mapped out and shaped our Lives even before we were born into this world, that is the reason; as a youth, you need to give your life to the Divine Godhead and also to His Principles and Patterns; so as to fit in well with His divine purpose for your life. Jeremiah 1:4-9 says the word of the LORD came to me, saying, "Before I formed you in the womb I knew you, before you were born I set you apart; I appointed you as a prophet to the nations." "Ah, Sovereign LORD," I said, "I do not know how to speak; I am only a child." But the LORD said to me, "Do not say, 'I am only a child.' You must go to everyone I send you to and say whatever I command you. Do not be afraid of them, for I am with you and will rescue you," declares the LORD. Then the LORD reached out his hand and touched my mouth and said to me, "Now, I have put my words in your mouth." Jeremiah 29:11 for I know the plans I have for you," declares the LORD, "plans to prosper you and not to harm you, plans to give you hope and a future.

Exodus 20:12 Honour your father and your mother, so that you may live long in the land the LORD your God is giving you (remember only in the Lord) in as much as our parents are telling us what is right; we need to obey. You know that when the kingdom of the anti-Christ comes in its most complete manifestation on earth, the world will say to the Youth, "Do not obey your parents, especially if those parents are teaching you about God and about Jesus Christ. They do not know what is best for you anyway. Must children obey the government? Yes; we have to obey the government of our various countries. But that does not rule out obeying our parents. In fact, obeying government begins by obeying our parents. Our parents are the form of government nearest to us.

But even now Satan tells you to disobey your parents, doesn't he, Youth? Sometimes he uses the world's philosophies and attitudes to tell us that: "Just do it." Or, "Don't worry about the consequences, be happy. Just do it and you will be happy." Children and young people, you don't need to swallow that Satan's argument, do you? Or he uses our friends. They say to us: "But do it just this once. Your mom and dad will never know if you do it just once." Or Satan uses an older brother or sister, who set a bad example for you. You want to be like them, to do what they do. Whatever the means Satan uses, he is deceiving you; because, what comes after six are more than seven; just like when he came to Eve in the Garden of Eden and asked, "Did God really say that? Perhaps God doesn't know what is best, and doesn't know what will really make you happy!" That is the approach that he uses today too. Not what Satan wants, but what God wants, the text tells us. God is our Creator and Saviour, so God must be obeyed. And God says, Children, obey your parents; only in the divine will of God.

The commandment reminds us, as a Youth, that your parents have authority over you. Your brother does not. Your sister does not.

And your friend down the street does not. They have no business telling you what to do unless Mom and Dad specifically appointed them for a time to be your babysitter. Apart from that, they do not. But your parents do have authority over you. God gave them that authority; and He gave them the wisdom, knowledge, and spiritual zeal to bring you up in a godly way. Therefore He commands us to obey our parents in the Lord; in the Will of God Ephesians 6:1, Proverb 6:20, 23:22.

By implication, He also commands us to obey those who stand in the place of our parents. Especially this means our teachers. When parents send their children to school, they entrust the care and learning of their child to the teacher; they give that teacher authority to teach their child as needed. Parents, do you insist on it that your children obey their teachers? For teachers stand in our place to teach good things in schools! If we undermine the authority of our teachers, we teach our child to disregard our own authority!

The command now is to obey. What is obedience? That answer is easy. Obedience is, first of all, doing what you are told; and secondly, doing what you are told willingly and submissively. "Children, obey your parents in the Lord ...," must also be understood to mean, you must obey your parents if your parents' command is not against the Word of God. If they ask you to do that which comes against Scripture, then you must obey God's Word. Jesus says in Matthew 10:37, "He that love father or mother more than me is not worthy of me ..."

In Matthew 10:26-40 Jesus said that he didn't come to bring peace but a sword. He said that at times he would divide parents from their children and children from their parents. Those are the exceptional cases, yet; Children can only obey positive directions John 2:1-5.

The whole assumption of this passage in this book is that Godly parents have enough Biblical knowledge to administer the home with

Godly principles and patterns. They must give positive, reasonable, clear directions to their children in order to admit the command that pleases the Lord. Read all these Scriptures for your benefits.

Joshua 1: 7-9

Be strong and very courageous. Be careful to obey all the law my servant Moses gave you; do not turn from it to the right or to the left, that you may be successful wherever you go. 8 Do not let this Book of the Law depart from your mouth; meditate on it day and night, so that you may be careful to do everything written in it. Then you will be prosperous and successful. 9 Have I not commanded you? Be strong and courageous. Do not be terrified; do not be discouraged, for the LORD your God will be with you wherever you go

1 Samuel 15:23

Rebellion is as bad as the sin of witchcraft, and stubbornness is as bad as worshipping idols.

Proverbs 3:5-6. Trust in the LORD with all your heart and lean not on your own understanding; in all your ways acknowledge him, and he will make your paths straight.

Proverbs 1:8-9 Listen, my son, to your father's instruction and do not forsake your mother's teaching. They will be a garland to grace your head and a chain to adorn your neck.

Proverbs 1:10 my son, if sinners entice you, do not give in to them.

Proverbs 17:25 A foolish son brings grief to his father and bitterness to the one who bore him.

Proverbs 23:22 Listen to your father, who gave you life, and do not despise your mother when she is old.

Proverbs 8:32-33 now then, my sons, listen to me; blessed are those who keep my ways. Listen to my instruction and be wise; do not ignore it.

Proverbs 20:11 Even a child is known by his doings, whether his work is pure, and whether it be right.

Proverbs 28:24 He who robs his father or mother and says, "It's not wrong"— he is a partner to him who destroys.

Song of Solomon gives an advice to the youth: 'Oh let me warn you, sisters in Jerusalem: Don't excite love, don't stir it up, until the time is ripe—and you're ready'. This is to tell the youth to be sober and serious and keep themselves pure in all their relationship. A youth needs to lay in his heart that he or she does not need more than one person to love and to behold in life and until the right time comes; do not do readily before you're ready. This is always better and even the best way in living out our purpose on earth.

Isaiah 40:29-31

He gives strength to the weary and increases the power of the weak. Even youths grow tired and weary, and young men stumble and fall, but those who hope in the LORD will renew their strength. They will soar on wings like eagles; they will run and not grow weary, they will walk and not be faint.

Micah 6:8, He has shown you … what is good. And what does the LORD require of you? Is to act justly and to love mercy and to walk humbly with your God.

Matthew 26:41 Watch and pray so that you will not fall into temptation.

Mark 12:29-31 The most important Law is this: and he answered 'Hear, O Israel, and 'Hear, and also O Youth, hear this, the Lord our God, the Lord is one. Love the Lord your God with all your heart and with all your soul and with your entire mind and with all your strength. 'The second is this: 'Love your neighbour as yourself. 'There is no commandment greater than these."

1 Corinthians 10:13 No temptation has seized you except what is common to man. And God is faithful; he will not let you be tempted beyond what you can bear. But when you are tempted, he will also provide a way out so that you can stand up under it. A genuine Youth that wants to live into God's principle and Pattern and make Heaven at the end of this terrible world, and even want to get to the stage of elderhood enrichment; need to take heed to all these Words of God and Advice in the bible.

Ephesians 6:1-3. Do what your parents tell you. This is only right. 'Honour your father and mother' is the first commandment that has a promise attached to it, namely, 'so you will live well and have a long life.

Colossians 3:20. Children, obey your parents in everything, for this pleases the Lord.

James 1:13 When tempted, no one should say, "God is tempting me." For God cannot be tempted by evil, nor does he tempt anyone

James 2:14-17. What good is it, my brothers, if a man claims to have faith but has no deeds? Can such faith save him? Suppose a brother or sister is without clothes and daily food. If one of you says to him, "Go, I wish you well; keep warm and well fed," but does nothing about his physical needs, what good is it? In the same way, faith by itself, if it is not accompanied by action, is dead. That is to say, as a Youth, when you confesses God and faith in Him you need to back it up by action or be the doers of His Word in purity and Holiness.

1 Timothy 4:12 don't let anyone look down on you because you are young but set an example for the believers in speech, in life, in love, in faith, and in purity.

1Timothy 5:1-2 do not speak harshly to an older man, but speak to him as to a father, to younger men as brothers, to older women as mothers, to younger women as sisters - with absolute purity.

2 Timothy 2:22-25 run away from infantile indulgence. Run after mature righteousness—faith, love, peace—joins those who are in honest and serious prayer before God. Refuse to get involved in inane discussions; they always end up in fights. God's servant must not be argumentative, but a gentle listener and a teacher who keeps cool, working firmly but patiently with those who refuse to obey.

1 Peter 5:5-9 tell us to be submissive to those who are older. All of you clothe yourselves with humility toward one another, because, "God opposes the proud but gives grace to the humble." Humble yourselves, therefore, under God's mighty hand, that he may lift you up in due time. Cast all your anxiety on him because he cares for you. Be self-controlled and alert. Your enemy the devil prowls around like a roaring lion looking for someone to devour. Resist him, standing firm in the faith, because you know that your brothers throughout the world are undergoing the same kind of sufferings. In this particular scripture, we are all brother and sister in the Family of the Divine Godhead;

We need to respect ourselves and respond to abilities of been our brother's keeper, and also, I suggest to the youth to enlist themselves with a godly elders, it could be their godparent, guardian, and mentor, and always fervent and busy for the Lord in Evangelisms, ministering in the Church; in Music section, Drama, Crusade and retreats, good games such as football, Swimming, learning Languages and musical instruments etc. and also flock together only with genuine children of God always busy with your hand in good work by so doing; you will avoid and escape some youthful lust and sexual gravity and do all these will definitely navigate you and link you up with divine current of Holy Spirit your best companion and the great enabler of your purpose on earth. Avoid a picture you cannot control, always fervent in prayers ask God for anything, I mean all things; He is your Creator and makes sure you hear His answers towards your questions. Consider the end before you begin, many young ones and even adults play with youthful Lust and impurity; then console themselves that all is well, everything is going on fine with them, it seems they are happy for the moment of which the world, Sin and Devil flash on them. But remember, sinful pleasure dies in your grasp. It end is crunching, bitter, and eternal in consequences. Be wise, believe the Bible and learn from the experience of the fallen Romans 6:1, 15.

No matter whom you are or what you have done, God loves you and He cares about you, so "Live for Him." Is always for your Good and Benefits Roman 8:28, 30. Ephesian1:11, 1Peter 2:9, Hebrew 9:15. Finally, I will like to suggest to all Young ones and adult youth to be conversant with the books of Proverbs, Ecclesiastes Roman and Timothy.

BAPTISM

Baptism, like the Lord's Supper, was transformed in both meaning and content by our Lord Jesus Christ. Baptism became not only a repentance for one's sins but being baptized in the name of the Trinity now also assured forgiveness and incorporation into the Body of Christ, the Church. Baptism was the once and for all initiatory rite whereby one received the Holy Spirit and came into the Church. (Not Denominational or individual ministry thing)

The New Testament gives fascinating clues as to how the Early Church practiced baptism. However, there is no "Handbook on Baptism" in the New Testament. We can only surmise the proper form and meaning of baptism based on various verses that mention the doctrines. Some of those verses are referenced in the table below.

"…in a few days, you will be baptized with the Holy Spirit." – are water baptism and baptism of the Holy Spirit two separate things? Does one follow the other? Acts 1:4 - 1:5, "All of them were filled with the Holy Spirit …" Acts 2:1 - 2:41, "The promise is for you and your children …" -sometimes used to justify infant baptism Acts 2:38 – 2:39

The late 1st-century/early-2nd century Epistle of Barnabas (possibly written by the Apostle) contains the following description of Christian baptism:

The Teaching of the Twelve Apostles describes fasting before baptism ceremony; of which I remember, I was asked to fast for three days in Church Vestry, before I was baptized as a member of the Apostolic church and of which I am suggesting that it is of great privileges for baptismal candidates to go through some Biblical fundamental or basics Teaching before admission into the Body of Christ.

Baptism was related to Jewish purification ceremonies but was made as a Covenant by Jesus. He commanded disciples to be baptized as the sign and seal of initiation into His church (similar to circumcision being the rite of entry into the Old Covenant community). Baptism signified regeneration but was not confused with the conversion. Some were baptized but later shown to be unconverted. Baptism in the book of Acts took place directly upon profession of faith (Acts 2:41, 8:36-39, 9:18, 10:47, 48 etc). Baptism was to be with water but the mode is not specified in the NT. It was to be in the name of the Father, Son, and Spirit. It was administered to a person only once. While most baptisms recorded in the NT were adults. And also, it is worthy and acceptable in the body of Christ to run a fundamental belief and doctrine with all candidates before baptism into the body of Christ. (Church)

PERSONAL TESTIMONY

In 1983, my father was called by our Residential Pastor then, and I discovered that there was a discussion of sort divine direction that I must be baptized, after which I was enrolled for fundamental belief and doctrine in the bible for some Weeks. After the studies, I was baptized in a pool of water carved behind the Sanctuary; though I was the only candidate and after the baptism, the pool was open to flow away. There again 1997, I was asked by another church denomination to re-baptized and it became a misunderstanding. Therefore, I went to God in prayer and this was the revelation the Spirit of God gave to me — In the revelation, I was sitting in my childhood congregation with a fine white clothing and at same time I saw my old and unattractive Flesh and Figure of mine in the pool of water I was baptized with inside the church and I saw a man unfamiliar walking on space without shoe on, that is; he is not moving on a ground; it was like three platform off the ground. As he was moving, he was preaching and he was keep mentioning -we have talked about the Death of Christ; we are now talking about the Resurrection of Christ … … 3x and I woke up. That's to me; going back inside that Pool is like picking the old nature and or it shows that my first baptism was fully accepted by God and one of the reasons for baptism is to the Body of Christ not denominational church or individual ideas and it should be done once.

LORD'S SUPPER

The Lord's Supper or the Lord Table is a reminder of what Jesus did in the past, a symbol of our present relationship with him and a promise of what he will do in the future. Let's examine these three aspects.

The bread and wine are to remind us of Jesus' death on the cross (Luke 22:19-20; 1 Cor. 11:26). In the Lord's Supper, we individually eat a piece of bread in remembrance of Jesus. When we drink the "fruit of the vine," we remember that Jesus' blood was shed for us and that it signifies the new covenant. The Lord's Supper looks back to the death of Jesus Christ on the cross.

The Lord's Supper also pictures our present relationship with Jesus Christ. The crucifixion has a continuing significance to all who have taken up a cross to follow Jesus. We continue to participate in his death (Rom. 6:4; Gal. 2:20; Col. 2:20) because we participate in his life (Gal. 2:20; Eph. 2:6; Col. 2:13; 3:1).

Paul wrote, "Is not the cup of thanksgiving for which we give thanks a participation in the blood of Christ? And is not the bread that we break a participation in the body of Christ?" (1 Cor. 10:16). With the Lord's Supper, we show that we share in Jesus Christ. We participate with him, commune with him, and become united in him. The Lord's Supper helps us look upward, to Christ.

In John 6, Jesus used bread and wine to graphically illustrate our need to be spiritually nourished by him: "Unless you eat the flesh of the Son of Man and drink his blood, you have no life in you. ... Whoever eats my flesh and drinks my blood remains in me, and I in him" (verses 53-56). The Lord's Supper reminds us that real life is found only in Jesus Christ, with him living in us.

The Lord's Supper is rich in meaning. That is why it has been an important part of the Christian tradition throughout the centuries. Sometimes it has become a lifeless observance, done more out of habit than with meaning. Some people overreact by stopping the doctrine entirely. The better response is to restore the meaning. And it is even unto our own peril if we take it unworthily; because it is just as if we are nailing Him to the cross at second time 1Peter 2:24. It somehow amazed me when some individual that are living in open sin as such that are not to be heard or mention among true Bodies of Christ still go ahead and partake of it.

Does the Scripture prescribe a correct frequency observance to us Christians the Spiritual Israelites? Some churches commemorate Jesus' death every week; some monthly; others quarterly. Some do it annually. At least one preacher has argued that the Lord's Supper should be taken only once each year. He gave three reasons for an annual observance; not anyone is welcome to observe the service, though; children likely to be in the service during the time of old practice of the Passover, but children might not partake, one of the elements of the Passover feast was bitter herbs Exodus 12:8-11 – This is not something that small children were likely to have been able to eat, that is why God told the adult that if their children that are present asked them the meaning of what they are doing; that is Passover, they should explain to their children of it.

I remembered when I was at young age in my childhood church, if you are not up to certain age you may not partake of Lord Supper and or; the minister would make announcement that if you know you are living in sin please, quietly go out of the church which after they will close the three entrance of the church both the sinners and small children would stay outside the church and wait for their individual family.

In order to answer those that argue about children partake the Lord's Supper, we must use the examples and commands given to us under the new covenant. While some similarities can be made between the Passover and the Lord's Supper, they each have their own unique purpose and commands. The Lord's Supper is to be observed on the first day of the week Acts 20:7, and we are to partake of the fruit of the vine and unleavened bread Luke 22:14-20. The Lord's Supper should only be eaten by the born again Christians because when we do, we are in communion with Christ.

Literally, the cup of blessing which we bless, is it not the communion of the blood of Christ? "And the blessing we both share under His divine atonement for all." The bread which we break, is it not the communion of the body of Christ for us? Though; many are we, yet; one body of Christ; for we all partake of that one bread the Word of God; and Wine His divine bloodshed for our atonement. 1 Corinthians 10:16 Act 2:41-47.

You cannot find an example in the New Testament where a child or a non-Christian partook of the Lord's Supper. Unlike the Passover, which was eaten by the household, and still, we could not even justify if children in the household in ancient time were able to partake? The Lord's Supper is taken when the Christians are gathered together to form the body of Christ. This same idea is true when it comes to partaking of the Lord's Supper Since the Lord's Supper is for Christians it excludes our children from partaking of it. The reason I say this is because under the new covenant we must choose to become a Christian, which means we must know what we are doing. We must be mature in Christ and all things pertaining to Christ that is why the very first set of people He had it with were The

First Twelve Apostles and they are the one He gave the command to this practice in remembrance of Him.

We learn three things about the purpose of the Lord's Supper from the following verses:

1 Corinthians 11:23 For I received from the Lord that which I also delivered to you: that the Lord Jesus on the same night in which He was betrayed took bread; [24] and when He had given thanks, He broke it and said, "Take, eat; this is My body which is broken for you; do this in remembrance of Me." [25] In the same manner, He also took the cup after supper, saying, "This cup is the new covenant in my blood. These do, as often as you drink it, in remembrance of me." [26] For as often as you eat this bread and drink this cup, you proclaim the Lord's death till He comes. [27] Therefore whoever eats this bread or drinks this cup of the Lord in an unworthy manner will be guilty of the body and blood of the Lord. [28] But let a man examine himself, and so let him eat of the bread and drink of the cup. [29] For he who eats and drinks in an unworthy manner eats and drinks judgment to himself, not discerning the Lord's body.

First, we are supposed to partake of it in remembrance of Jesus. Just as the Passover was a reminder to the Jews of how death passed over them, which led to their freedom of slavery, the Lord's Supper reminds us of how Jesus made eternal salvation possible for us by becoming the perfect sacrifice on the cross so we could have freedom from the bondage of sin.

Second, when we partake of the Lord's Supper, we proclaim His death until He comes again (vs. 26). Children might not eat the Jewish Passover; however, the point is that children (boys) were circumcised on the eighth day. Therefore Jewish children (male or female) entered the religious congregation at birth. The following shows that circumcised children might eat, but an uncircumcised adult visitor could not: Even when our children do not partake of the

Lord's Supper, when they see us partaking they may eventually ask us why we do it, and we can use that opportunity to teach them about what it represents without them partaking of it. Teaching children about God are important. Is like giving Christ to them early enough so that as they are growing; they grow in Him as to able to choose life instead of death.

The first hour and instance of this blessed Remembrance of Christ were with The Twelve apostle and he took bread, and when he had given thanks, he broke it and gave it to them, saying, "This is my body, which is given for you. Do this in remembrance of me." 20 And likewise, the cup after they had eaten, saying, "This cup that is poured out for you is the new covenant in my blood. And when the hour came, he reclined at table and the apostles with him. And he said to them, "I have earnestly desired to eat **this Passover** with you before I suffer. For I tell you I will not eat it until it is fulfilled in the kingdom of God." And **he took a cup**, and when he had given thanks he said, "Take this, and divide it among yourselves. 18 For I tell you that from now on I will not drink of the fruit of the vine until the kingdom of God comes." to me; – the partakers of the Lord table should be among the true Christians and Mature ones in the things and body of Christ.

Third, we learn that partaking of the Lord's Supper is a time of reflection (vs. 28). We need to examine how we are living our lives in accordance with God's will. When we stop and think about the significance of the Lord's Supper, it becomes a reminder for us each week to live pure and holy lives before God. It is important that we know what we are doing as we partake of Lord's Supper so we do not partake of it in an unworthy manner as the Corinthians did 1 Cor. 11:17-22

Paul states that we will be guilty of Jesus' blood and His body if we partake of it in an unworthy manner (vs. 29). While our children can not go through motions of eating the bread and drinking the fruit of the vine, is because they cannot fully understand what they are doing. Therefore, they cannot partake of the Lord's Supper in a worthy manner. If they are old enough to understand the significance of the Lord's Supper and everything that goes with it, then they are old enough to become Christians.

In conclusion, while we can learn much from the Old Testament, we cannot use it to justify what we do under the New Testament. The Jews under the Old Testament were commanded to observe the Passover with their household, but Christians are commanded to partake of the Lord's Supper together when they worship God on the first day of the week. While we should encourage our children to pray, give, sing, and listen to the preacher, we must not allow them to partake of the Lord's Supper until they become Christians because they need to know what they are doing so they can partake of it in a worthy manner. The Bible clearly requires active self-examination of all who would partake of the Lord's Supper.

Neither the uninstructed nor those who do not consciously recognize their own sinfulness and utter unworthiness apart from Christ's atoning work on the cross should approach the Lord's Table. What have we learned so far from the OT Passover feast which Jesus was celebrating in the evening He instituted it is what we call The Lord's Supper?

The Passover was a remembrance feast celebrated in Exodus as the result of deliverance from Egyptian slavery. If children would ask about its meaning they should be told the Exodus story. Those participating had to be circumcised. Proper cleansing and sanctification had to take place, a complete turnaround to the Lord, a deep conversion experience.

As we strive to pass down to our children, "the faith once for all delivered to the saints" (Jude 3). Covenantal training by parents, and through Sunday school and Fundamental belief classes we can prepare our youth for public profession of faith, and equip them for a life of service to God. The Lord Supper should not be administered in other to prevent sin or fall

There was a definite time — a definite hour — when He held this supper, setting us an example ... It was 'when the hour was come,' Luke 22:14 that Jesus first introduced the bread and the wine." And there will come a certain time He will eat it again with us in God's kingdom Luke 22:16/30.

Jesus changed the way we observe "the ordinance of the Passover for New Testament times ... We take unleavened bread, symbolizing his broken body, and the wine, symbolizing his shed blood, as a remembrance, looking back to his death ... The time for commemorating Passover ... is once a year. Jesus set us an example 1 Peter 2:21, observing it at this set time once a year Luke 2:42.

We do it in remembrance of the Lord's death — a remembrance of His death. And momentous occasions are always observed annually, once a year, on the anniversary of the event they commemorate."

The Lord's Supper is for people who have faith in Jesus Christ as Lord and Saviour, those who have forsaken the world, the Sin, and its Lusts since they have been baptized, called out from the darkness into the marvellous light of Christ Jesus 1Peter 2:9. We need to tell people that the bread and wine are for those who have faith in Christ. They must make their own decision as to whether to partake.

Blessed are we, when we are the doer of the Word and fulfil all the requirement and commandment of His divine principles and practices/patterns therein Matthew 7:21, James 1:22, Jeremiah 11:6, Roman 2:13

MINISTRY

Leadership in the Early Church were people with divine calling from God Almighty, divine appointment into Offices of Christ and Holy Spirit Gifts; they are full of Grace, and fruits of Holy Spirit Act 6:3, Exodus 18:21.

The early church was extremely egalitarian in nature. They meet every first day of the week since our Lord Jesus Christ resurrected on this particular day it become seemly for the Apostle and the early church to meet together daily in Apostle Doctrine, breaking of bread and sharing in love. Though the God Almighty of the Sabbath still blesses Sabbath gathering, no day in the presence of God that which is not bless and relevant; provided we gather unto Him alone in His Divine Word, principles, and Patterned and also follow His ways and precepts.

Every baptized member was seen to have a gift (see Rom 12:4-8, 1 Pet 4:10-11, 1 Corinthians 12:1-31, 1 Corinthians 14:26, Ephesian 4:11-13). But in time, some formal positions of church leadership evolved, probably because of the ever-increasing size of the congregations. Congregations are exhorted several times in the New Testament to obey and submit to their leaders:

"Obey your leaders and submit to their authority. They keep watch over you as men who must give an account." Hebrew 13:17; see also 1 Thessalonica 5:12-13 and 1Timothy 5:17

"The Apostles have preached to us from the Lord Jesus Christ; Jesus Christ from God ... And thus preaching through countries and cities, they appointed the first fruits of their conversion to be bishops and ministers over such as should afterwards believe, having first proved them by the Spirit ... So likewise our Apostles knew of our Lord Jesus Christ, that there should contentions arise, upon account of the ministry. And therefore having a perfect fore-knowledge of this, they appointed persons, and then gave direction, how, when they should choose and approved men to succeed in their ministry."

Below we discuss the different "church officials" that appeared in the first-century church below.

Apostles

The first custodians of the early church were the apostles – and more specifically, the "The Twelve" chosen by Jesus. The word "apostle" comes from the Greek word Apostolos that means:

"A delegate; specifically an ambassador of the Gospel; officially a commissioner of Christ ("apostle"), (with miraculous powers):—apostle, messenger, he that is sent. (Strong's Hebrew and Greek Dictionaries)

Immediately before His ascension, Christ instructs his remaining 11 apostles to carry on his ministry:

"[8]But you will receive power when the Holy Spirit comes on you, and you will be my witnesses in Jerusalem, and in all Judea and Samaria, and to the ends of the earth." Acts 1:8

> After the ascension, the 11 remaining apostles wished to replace Judas Iscariot, and decided that a prime qualification for the replacement apostle was to have participated in Jesus' earthly ministry from the start:

Therefore it is necessary to choose one of the men who have been with us the whole time the Lord Jesus went in and out among us, beginning from John's baptism to the time when Jesus was taken up from us. For one of these must become a witness with us of his resurrection." Acts 1:21-22

Matthias (never to be heard from again in the New Testament) was chosen as the Judas-replacement.

However, the original twelve plus Matthias are not the only apostles referred to in the New Testament. Paul & Barnabas (Acts 14:14), Andronicus and Junias (Rom 16:7) and, possibly, James the brother of Jesus (Gal 1:19) also receive the appellation.

The reference to Junias as an apostle in Romans 16:7 is interesting because Junias is the feminine form of a Greek name (see below). Depending on how one interprets the passage (is it saying that Andronicus and Junias are well known to the apostles, or that they are outstanding apostles?), we may have grounds to identify a female apostle. "Greet Andronicus and Junias, my relatives who have been in prison with me. They are outstanding among the apostles, and they were in Christ before I was." Junias (Iounias) is clearly of the feminine form, as Thayer's Greek Definitions states:

A Christian woman at Rome, mentioned by Paul as one of his kinsfolk and fellow prisoners, the issue of Junias was the same like that of Aquila and Priscilla and that does not give a woman license to be an office Apostle or parade herself into Spiritual Leadership and Authority.

Bishop (or overseer)

Next in importance to the apostles were the bishops (or overseers) and the elders. The term bishop comes from the Greek word episkopos:

"A superintendent, that is, a Christian officer in general charge of an (or the) church (literally or figuratively):—bishop, overseer." (Strong's Hebrew and Greek Dictionaries)

In the New Testament, bishops are instructed to be "shepherds of the church of God"

Keep watch over yourselves and all the flock of which the Holy Spirit has made you overseers. Be shepherds of the church of God, which he bought with his own blood." Acts 20:28

The qualifications to be a bishop are sharp:

"[1]Here is a trustworthy saying: If anyone sets his heart on being an overseer, he desires a noble task. [2]Now the overseer must be above reproach, the husband of but one wife, temperate, self-controlled, respectable, hospitable, able to teach, [3]not given to drunkenness, not violent but gentle, not quarrelsome, not a lover of money. [4]He must manage his own family well and see that his children obey him with proper respect. [5](If anyone does not know how to manage his own family, how can he take care of God's church?) [6]He must not be a recent convert, or he may become conceited and fall under the same judgment as the devil. [7]He must also have a good reputation with outsiders so that he will not fall into disgrace and into the devil's trap." (NIV, 1 Tim 3:1-7)

See also Philippians 1:1 and 1 Titus 1:5-9. Bishops of churches founded by the apostles were said to be in succession to the apostles.

Elder (or presbyter)

The term "elder" comes from the Greek word presbuteros. Both "presbyter" and "priest" are derived from this word. According to Strong's:

"Comparative of presbus (elderly); older; as a noun, a senior; specifically an Israelite Sanhedrist (also figuratively, a member of the celestial council) or Christian "presbyter":—elder (-est), old." (Strong's Hebrew and Greek Dictionaries)

The term is used in two different ways in the New Testament, depending upon whether it is used in reference to the Jerusalem Church or the Gentile church. In the former, the concept of the elder was modelled after the Old Testament pattern, with elders acting as a decision-making council in the Jerusalem church (see Acts 15, Acts 21:17-26). The term as we use it today comes from the Gentile church, and is often used to denote the highest official in a particular church or area:

Paul and Barnabas appointed elders for them in each church and, with prayer and fasting, committed them to the Lord, in whom they had put their trust." (Acts 14:23)

The qualifications for elders are similar to the aforementioned ones for bishop. In fact, one could read Titus 1:5-9 as indicating that there was no distinction between bishops (overseers) and elders in the 1st-century church:

"[5]The reason I left you in Crete was that you might straighten out what was left unfinished and appoint elders in every town, as I directed you. [6]An elder must be blameless, the husband of but one wife, a man whose children believe and are not open to the charge of being wild and disobedient. [7]Since an overseer is entrusted with God's work, he must be blameless—not overbearing, not quick-tempered, not given to drunkenness, not violent and not pursuing dishonest gain. [8]Rather he must be hospitable, one who loves what is good, who is self-controlled, upright, holy and disciplined. [9]He must hold firmly to the trustworthy message as it has been taught so that he can encourage others by sound doctrine and refute those who oppose it." (Titus 1:5-9). See also James 5:14-15, 1 Tim 4:14, and 1 Peter 5:1-4 for other references to elders.

Adding further to the hierarchy of the first-century church (were bishops and elders on the same level?), the apostles sometimes referred to themselves as elders – John refers to himself simply as "the elder" in 2 John 1:1 and 3 John 1:1.

Deacons

Finally, we have the deacon, which comes from the Greek word *diakonos*, often translated as "servant":

"An attendant, that is, (generally) a waiter (at the table or in other menial duties); specifically a Christian teacher and or what we can terms as an assistant pastor (technically a deacon or deaconess):— deacon, minister, servant." (Strong's Hebrew and Greek Dictionaries)

Traditionally, the first deacons were seven Hellenistic Jewish Christians chosen by the apostles to assist in the "daily distribution of food" to the poor:

"They chose Stephen, a man full of faith and of the Holy Spirit; also Philip, Procorus, Nicanor, Timon, Parmenas, and Nicolas from Antioch, a convert to Judaism." Acts 6:5

Stephen has the distinction of being the first martyr in the history of the church (his murder being aided and abetted by one Saul of Tarsus).

The qualifications to be a deacon are similar to those of being a bishop or elder – with the distinction that there is no requirement to have the gift of teaching:

"[8]Deacons, likewise, are to be men worthy of respect, sincere, not indulging in much wine, and not pursuing dishonest gain. [9]They must keep hold of the deep truths of the faith with a clear conscience.

¹⁰They must first be tested; and then if there is nothing against them, let them serve as deacons. ¹¹In the same way, their wives are to be women worthy of respect, not malicious talkers but temperate and trustworthy in everything. ¹²A deacon must be the husband of but one wife and must manage his children and his household well. ¹³Those who have served well gain an excellent standing and great assurance in their faith in Christ Jesus." (NIV, 1 Tim 3:8-13)

By the end of the first century, deacons assisted church leaders, managed the church treasury, and served the needs of the poor. In time, they also assisted in Holy Communion such as baptism. (But not administer).

Both women and men served as deacons in the early church, as can be seen by the Phoebe mentioned by Paul in Romans 16:1-2. The NIV translates it as follows:

"¹I commend to you our sister Phoebe, a servant of the church in Cenchrea. ²I ask you to receive her in the Lord in a way worthy of the saints and to give her any help she may need from you, for she has been a great help to many people, including me." Romans 16:1-2,

The word that the NIV (and KJV) translates as "servant" is actually from the Greek word diakonos, defined above (the NIV has a note which gives an alternative translation of diakonos as "deaconess").

In 1984, I was prayed for by the Auction of the Holy Spirit of God by the Presbyters into a Children Sunday School Teacher, Soul Winning Team and Youth Group of which by the special grace of God till today I am still on that line.

RELATIONSHIP

Ecclesiastes 4:9-12, 1Samuel 18:1-3, Roman 12:15, John 15:12-15.

FRIENDSHIP

True friendship is the one, in which the individuals do not have to maintain formalities with each other. Sharing true friendship is the situation when the person you are talking about is counted as one among your Family members when the relationship you share with him/her reaches a stage that even if you don't correspond for sometimes, your friendship remains intact. Best friends need not meet up often to make sure that the friendship remains constant. Ecclesiastes 4:9-10.

The trust between best friends is such that if one friend falls in trouble, the other will not think twice to help. If the bond between two friends is strong, true friends can endure even long distances. For them, geographical separation is just a part of life. True friendship is perhaps the only relation that survives the trials and tribulations of time and remains unconditional. A unique blend of affection, loyalty, love, respect trust and loads of fun is perhaps what describes the true meaning of friendship. Similar interests, mutual respect and strong attachment with each other are what friends share between each other.

These are just the general traits of a friendship. To experience what is friendship, one must have true friends, who are indeed a rare treasure. Friendship is a feeling of comfort and emotional safety with a person.

It is when you do not have to weigh your thoughts and measure words, before your friend. It is when someone knows you better than yourself and assures to be your side in every emotional crisis. It is when you can sleep fighting and get another morning with a better understanding. Friendship is much beyond roaming together and sharing good moments; it is when someone comes to rescue you from the worst phase of life Friendship are eternal. Different people have different definitions of friendship. For some, it is the trust in an individual that he/she won't hurt you. For others, it is unconditional love.

There are some who feel that friendship is companionship. People from definitions based on the kind of experiences they have had. This is one relation that has been nurtured since time immemorial.

There are famous stories about friends in traditions of different religions all over the world. They say a person who has found a faithful friend has found a priceless treasure. Psychologically speaking, friendship may be defined as 'a dynamic, mutual relationship between two individuals. This greatly helps in the emotional development of an individual.

However, any relation needs constant nurturing and development from all the people that are involved in one.

Friendship cannot survive if one person makes all the effort to sustain it without any mutual recognition from others. True friends don't desert each other when one is facing trouble. They would face it together and support each other, even if it is against the interests of the other person. Best friends don't analyse each other; they don't have to do so. They accept each other with their positive and negative qualities. Nothing is hidden between true friends. They know each other's strengths as well as weaknesses. One would not overpower the other. They would respect each other's individuality.

Different people have different tastes and temperaments and hence make different types of friends. They tend to bond with some and stay away from some. It is rightly said that "A friend to all is a friend to none". We tend to meet new people day in day out but out of those numerous people, we tend to be friends with only those who share some similar traits or attitudes. With time and growing trust, some people get really close to each other and remain true friends. They stand up for each other in times of need and provide full support when you lose confidence in yourself. 1Samuel 18:1-3

True friends are not opportunists. They don't help, because they have something to gain out of it. True friendship is marked by selflessness if you have even one true friend, consider yourself blessed. Remember, all best friends are friends, but not all friends can be best friends.

In this world of betrayers and backstabbers, there are still some people who are worth being friends with. They have to be recognized and respected for being best friends, for the lifetime. Since friendship starts the moment a child starts socializing, the kind of friends that the child chooses should be taken care of till the time he/she learns to differentiate between right and wrong. Wrong peers or lack of socializing can lead to severe psychological traumas and disorders, finally leading to social instability.

The correct peer group is essential for the development of the personality of a child. Both positive and negative experiences refine the personality of the individual. Thus it is essential that you find friends who are compatible with you on an emotional and psychological basis.

True friends are hard to find, most of the time, people land up with wrong people, who are difficult to adjust with. With the increasing selfishness and cut-throat competition between peers, it has become more difficult to find a person who can be blindly trusted and looked upon in need. Also, with increasing interest of people in gossip and cheap plots, betrayal of friendship has become very common.

One more reason because of which friendship these days do not bloom is self- engrossed nature of most of the people. Even worse are those cases, where betrayal of friendship is done for materialistic pleasures. Coping up with a broken friendship is quite hard, more so if you have no fault of yours. But, life goes on and you make new friends. You push away your hurtful past and learn a valuable lesson from it.

ACCEPT THE REALITY

When friends let you down and are not there for you when you need them the most, it's very heart wrenching. Sometimes the reason why friends betray you is just not known, which leaves you with a feeling of guilt that maybe something went wrong from your side.

In the case of betrayal, being at the receiving end leaves you hurt, confused and angry and you demand answers as to why have you been betrayed for absolutely no fault of yours; the talks end abruptly, phone calls are not returned, letters remain unanswered and there is no contact whatsoever. Hate it as much as you want, you will have to come to terms with reality and accept that things were not meant to be.

More note on Friendships;- Proverb 16:28, 17:9, 27:6, 17, 18:24, 22:24-25, 25:16-17, 27:5-6, 1Corithian 15:33.

MARRIAGE

In the beginning of the Bible God says, "It is not good for man to be alone." Genesis 2:18. He knows what is best for us, because He alone is the Author of Marriage and the True Divine Godhead alone can provide a "help-mate." Marriage is what He has instituted.

One of the life's most difficult decisions is to select the life partner with whom one would share the rest of his/her life. One mistake - and your life are miserable till the end of it. So, how to choose? Here are a few tips (Do not forget to read true life experience narrated at the end).

The most important thing is that you are meant to marry. Your hunt for a life partner should begin only when you decide to marry and you know very well that you are fully in Christ Jesus Matthew 6:33. Do not involve sexually with anyone before marriage - even if you are engaged to be married. There are so many complications which the world may consider as 'fashion' or a 'different lifestyle' - but are not moral, ethical, and acceptable before God and man, though; it may deem to be legal according to the laws of a country. Every sin that a person commits is outside the body, but the one who commits sexual immorality sins against one's own body. Your body is a holy temple where the Spirit of God should reside - do not defile it with the sin of adultery and destroy your holiness. However, marriage and sex after marriage are honourable and holy before God because

God has ordained that a man should cleave to his wife to raise godly offspring. Any other form of sexual relationships is sin and will be judged by God. Let not your youth claim for sinful lusts and misconduct before God. Conduct your body as a holy vessel for God's glory.

Before you go ahead to freeze upon the person who will be your spouse, pray and ask God to approve your choice. You really need to hear from Him and probably God will use any other method on Earth to confirm His divine direction to you. You need not accept people at a face value, rather; according to their inner man because charm is deceitful and beauty/Handsomeness is vain, But a Woman/Man who fears the LORD, He or She shall be praised Proverbs 31:30.

How wonderful would be the life of a young man or woman who sits in the presence of God before even starting off in the search for a life partner! Such a wise person would sit in the presence of God and read out the likes and dislikes before God and ask God to help in putting in the right things wisely because God is wiser than the wisest on earth. Then the wise person would pray for God to bring the right person into his or her life and reveal His will about the person at the right time. Then the wise person would pray to God, seeking His hand to work it to completion in marriage which would be honourable before man and God. And the wise person would pray along with his/her spouse, asking God to bless their holy matrimony to lead into a blessed family life, where they would live and glorify God throughout their walk together, remaining at the centre of God's will. A wise brother or a sister will commit everything to the hands of God to work it according to His Divine will, placing our desires about our life partner before Him.

We Christ-followers, need to pray unto God through His son Jesus Christ as He promised in His divine Word that no Man that Come unto him; will He cast out, when it comes to doing the will of God in anything pertaining to us we need to humbly go before Him and the Lord Jesus Christ and ask His divine Spirit to graciously revealed to us His divine Will and purpose in any way He chooses; because He is God of Thousands of Ways; when we have none. I find it apt to share with you some true life stories concerning a life partner of which they are of True life facts and not Grapevine

The first one was that of a brother who graduated from a University and for many years as an Architect there was no Job and he concluded that God was calling him to full-time ministry with this conclusion, he was wrong, for the fact that you are passing through some wilderness experience is not often mean to answer God's call into full-time ministry. It could be for you to draw closer to God in other to find out what needed to be done at that particular time. It was so in the life of this brother, though he was a faithful brother in the house of God in one of the Pentecostals churches at Alagbado Lagos, as a co-minister of the Word both in adults and Youth Bodies. With the assistance of one of the Elders in the church; thank God for Spirit-filled and genuine elders in the body of Christ; who went with this brother to a mountain called Mountain of Ikoyi (only Men were allowed to climb). On this faithful day when they got to the mountain, a prophet that did not know them before meet them at entrance of the mountain and prophesy to them that there was no need for them to start fasting and prayers, that; what the brother need to do is go back home and get married, this was a big surprise to both the elder and the brother. You see there is a way a genuine prophecy will agree with your inner man and instinct; they both went back and change their prayer point that God must reveal the right sister, to the glory of God; He that will never turn any man down, revealed a sister, a Ward of another elder. Since God was already involved it was confirmed to the sister and her guardian with another minister in other branch and within the period of two to three months the knot was tied, according to the testimony it was the senior pastor that gave out his new suit brought from abroad to this brother and the church segments contributes both in cash, raw food and kind to the success of the marriage. After three months or so; one of the elder (another elder precisely) called the brother to one of the Federal Projects in the Ministry of Works for one of the Lagos Estates Construction those days. After the project, God uses this project to bless the brother that he bought a Pick-up, a personal car and build a house of three bedrooms and two sets of a room and parlours at Lagos and his wife gave birth to Twins; these entire miracles happen within a year of settling down in divine directions to marriage in 1991/1992. God is ever faithful when you allowed Him and commits all to your Creator it is you that will gain and be happy at the end.

The Second story was that of a brother a grandson of well-known Pioneer and founder of a very Large Christian Organization the brother was a friend to sister B and sister M in this story also, but my early enlightenment in Christ never believe that if you are in children ministry you could be a terrible agent of Darkness, I believe that all children teachers must be a born again and clean Christians, but I was proved wrong with this story. The brother got a helping hand through one of our Children Executive elders, this elder was an elderly man; he just called the attention of this brother a friend to sister B and he asked him 'have you prayerfully considered sister M you about to settle down with? it was like what sort of question was this and the brother answered the elder this way: "she was a beautiful sister, humble always going about with a smile on her face and to him she look quiet' and seem to be a wife material it was then the elder said to brother T, we are going to pray and fast seven days about that; thank God the brother agreed; how many of our brother still earnestly and sincerely pray these days? May the good God save us? It was then brother T called the attention of sister B if she really knows sister M very well? She said well she cannot really say but she was a sister and she needed an assistance and she think she can offer the assistance to her as a believer and instantly brother T declared to sister B that he is not interested in the engagement with sister M again that himself and one of his daddy in the Lord had prayed and he really thank God that he prayed. Sister B could not get the message; the two sisters both left and went back to sister B place after much pleading with brother T. As from that day sister B started praying too; asking God why brother T decided to break the relationship. After all, it is because of him she came to Lagos though; she told sister B that it is because she had some problem with her aunt who she was staying with and that she wanted to stay on her own to start life, out of brotherly love and compassion sister B discussed with her pastor then she got a job with him of which both sister B and her pastor regretted, because she was the one that sent this pastor to bankruptcy by being a link between him and fraudsters. I remember that in one of the revelation God gave to me about this sister M; she told me that armed robbers were her brothers and in reality this was confirmed even then pastor had to called her attention and warned her concerning this – Yeah; spiritual wickedness always work hand in hands as the spirits of revenge always has a link with witchcrafts and witchcraft has a link with prostitution and armed robbery.

In reality, Holy Spirit of God make known of all secrets thank God brother T was delivered through Godly counsel, prayer, and determined obedience.

Many other true stories, I cannot relay in this book with you. What about another friend, a fervent brother, with anointing of a genuine evangelist, I remember children crusade we coordinated at Badagry so fruitful, his so called wife was also a sister in disguise, we were all in the children ministry, they both married, afterward, sister skilfully destroyed his life and later she packed out and married to another man outside the Faith entirely in another town and gave birth to Twins. This fervent brother died like a tortured madman; he was not easily accessible but was finally captured through the assistance of evil marriage with agent of darkness and I was told that one of the Pastors will go to this brother and warned him sometimes to be vigilant

Personal Experience: One of the insights I got about this brother marriage was not edifying at all and at the same time in that insight, I also, collected a key that belongs to me from his wife she was hiding this single key from me this was the way I saw it.

These three stories stated above made me answer those who asked if revelation is real or important before marriage.

Dear readers, if you cannot run asked who can carry you when it comes to issue of choosing spouse for marriage. "it is that very important', I suggest you needful and compulsorily have to hear your Creator either to go or not, the issue of marriage is not only for Sex or companionship, it is far deeper and with good meaning and reasons than that, brother you have to sleep deep' so that by the time you are fully awake you will know without a doubt and hesitation that this is your woman. Genesis 2:21.

We know from Genesis 2 that Adam was made before Eve. We also know that it was Adam who was told to keep The Garden and cultivate it. Part of God's command to Adam was to keep the Garden and to name the animals. This was not Eve's role. She was later made to be a helpmate to Adam and assist him in the calling God had given him, not the other way around. "For indeed man was not created for the woman's sake, but woman for the man's sake 1 Corinthian 11:9 The woman God Almighty destined for you; that's if you will allow Him to direct and lead you; will in many way Compliments your Vision, dream, Values and living purpose on Earth, I am telling you; that is one of the major reasons for marriage and as woman, a man God Almighty would bring you to you will every area of your Life fits for your living purpose and this would enable you to become a virtuous woman God ordain you to be Proverb 31:10-31.

At this point, I will like to advise and suggest to you not to deceive yourself when it comes to choosing Marriage partners or any other matter that will not only affect your entire life's and loved ones;

but will linger with you to eternity. Even, as a sister if you are truly convinced that someone belong to you, let the brother come with all conviction to propose to you and ask for your hand in marriage rather than fighting for what is not bidding, or that may never come to an existence and or; that which was just due to mere crushes – The issue of marriage is between you and God, God will only use every other method to confirm what is between you and Him; be it circumstances, Godly counsel, and prophecy. But I am telling you the Gospel Truth you must Pray, See, find and be Patient in other to receive from God. Even in the midst of His divine will for you there might be a period of "Oh God what is all these, is revelation real, can God be serious of what He is telling me"? And you could feel like quitting the counsels of God. All I can say is, "All things work together for good to those who love God.

"And also remember this, "If a child of God marries a child of the devil, he or she is certain to have trouble with his father-in-law." Proverbs 6:27-28

Jehovah Elohim is our Creator and He reign in all affair of His Creatures, He would not condemn the righteous and support wickedness of Men – that which belong to you He would give for your Joy and Happiness and to the Glory of His Holy Name Therefore, my advice to you, my dear friends, is: "Delight yourself in the LORD; and He shall give you the desires of your heart. Commit your way to the LORD; Trust in Him, And He shall bring it to pass." (The Bible - Psalm 37:4, 5) Every foundation built without Christ surely shall collapse. Jesus is the true love anyone could have in marriage without this you will just be managing to live. And also just make sure you hear from God 'Yes or GO ahead! This is a green light button worth living for.

This made me remember one of my auntie's friend story, she came to look for my aunt one day and met only me in the store, while she was sitting down she told me that her spirit man was telling her to ask me a question and I answered whoa!!, what is that question and she started to narrate to me how she lost a friend to her God's will in marriage; that she went to mountain to pray, before she came back a close friend of hers had taken over her man and some few month later they both left to London. I was like having this thought may be the man in question is not right for her, because you cannot go prayer and this happen, I was just thinking and the same time listening and she then mention that the man was still sending her money and gift and there was this particular digital camera she brought for my aunt to keep for her, she said the man sent it with some cash, but as she entered that very day her spirit just said, she should ask me if it is something she can collect, she also told me how the man was telling her most of the time that he has no peace in marriage with her betrayal friend and besides that, there was no single child between them for past 18 years and the first child of this my aunt friend with her in the store that day was a young lady about 18 years old preparing for WAEC Exam and it was even this man from London that sends the Exams money, and I asked what about her husband and the father of the young lady she said that was exactly the problem and reason for asking me for advice that the family of the man; her own husband went out to inquired, 'God knows where' that she was the cause who did not allow her husband to make it in life, that anywhere they go to they confirm the same thing and this make her too confused more as per she knows quite well she does not practice wickedness. It was then I was clear that the problem was from the wrong foundation of marriage, either we believe this or we forget it, a Woman is a treasure of blessings and fruitfulness to her rightful Man 1Peter 3:7, Hebrew 13:5, 1Timothy 6:6-7.

We have heard and see how people get massive improvement just because they come in contact with a rightful partner and how the most successful ones end up being paupers all just because of wrong relationships. As Mike Murdock put it; he said in one of his books that if a wrong people leave you; wrong thing stop happening. Read the whole chapter one (1) of the book of Jonah.

Dear friends, the issue of praying your way through in marriage is very compulsory if you want to sail peacefully on Earth to Heaven, no wonder Satan fight tooth and nail on this greater Part of Man on Earth. My aunt still not yet back, so I told her she should just ask for forgiveness of disobeying God in the first place, and back then; she should have intensified in praying to get her man instead of letting him go since the betrayal friend did not get married to the man and she even did elope with him to London with diabolical means, with prayers I believe; if it is true will of God for her she could have won her perfect will of God in marriage. And also, she told me that both the man and her friend were just living together in London for some time without legal agreement; and it was like when she got married to this her present husband the man in London then went to settle with her friend too. The bible made it clear that you cannot marry another man since the first man still living and since you both have married with a public witnesses of Heaven and Men, thereof, the marriage stand in the presence of God, no matter gestures of kindness he is trying to show to you just know that it is a trap of the devil to make you guilty of Adultery and no adulterer will make heaven Galatians 5:19-21, Revelation 21:7-8, 22:15, Exodus 20:14, Roman 8:5, 1Corinthian 6:9, Hebrew 13:4, then I told her to confess all that she had received and the digital camera gifts to her husband and she should also be in unity with her husband by allowing him to be a front in everything especially in the public, she thanked me and went away.

Marriage is for mature people; men and women (not boys and girls) who are able to form a separate family unit, independent both in finance and moral responsibility. There is only one ideal for marriage running right through the Scriptures, and that is one man joined to one woman. Genesis 2:1-18, Genesis 24: 1-end. Nowhere do we get the idea that we should try various partners before choosing the right one. We see that the selection of a partner was often made by parents, or sometimes as a reward, but the suggestion in the New Testament is the choice of two people to come together of their own free will; only in the will of the Lord.

Our natural desires can easily lead us into a wrong even dangerous position. Especially when we are young it is easy to become so convinced that we have found the right one that our judgement becomes blurred if not blind. There have been many who through an impetuous decision and infatuations led into a sad relationship or led away from a path of devotion to the Lord and obedience to His Word. It is not always advisable to marry because of some riches or materialism, I remember the era where you see girls and ladies doing some sorts of atrocities to get a man especially, with bankers and oil workers and if you asked them where you created from this man's ribs they instant answered you I am not born to suffer, I need to marry a man with a great affluence, even you may even discover some mothers assisting their daughters to go to any terrible length in achieving this. I remember a very close friend of mine from Uselu-Uku Delta State; in fact, this is one of the testimonies I love to share to youths that are ready for marriage and to let them know that God is still in the business of bringing a wife for His son and bringing a husband for His daughters. The Pastor of my Christian sister called her and asked her about her marriage life and she answered and said the man she saw in her insights was a young promising pastor (name withheld) but she is afraid because it's like she was older than him with two years, not knowing that the Parish Pastor called her for confirmation, because the said Pastor was having the same insights about her and he has discussed with his Pastor of their local church. But, there was a woman that wanted her daughter to marry my friend God's will; only God knows the reasons, but I am sure is one of those wrong motives; because God will not lead two sisters to one brother or brother to two sisters, it is not possible. 1 Corinthians

14:33, 40, 7:17 and these women gang up together with some other women in the church and did some terrible thing against my friend to the extent; this, my friend, will only gas as in messy in the public especially if the brother pastor is around there, she notice this but she cannot understand, dear friends a lot went with that sister I cannot relay here because is awful, do I want to talk about chicken pox on a her whole body they sent to attack her, just to separate her from the pastor; as they were doing one thing; they insist on another and it was like the pastor truly gave up on her and start relationship with this influential woman and her daughter.

This friend of mine was a lady of thirty-two years at that time in 1995. Then, we decided to go on serious prayers and God gave victory. A few days later this young pastor just runs down to her one evening around 5:00pm of one day and started pleading and asking this my sister to forgive him that many things were happening to him and he was told because he has dealt treacherously with the will of God for his life. It was later we were hearing that the woman and her daughter use to go to see an evil herbalist very early in the morning either with rooster or goat, and I am telling you God deal with that woman, her daughter and her family in His anger.

Another of my friend, now married she experience the same thing and in her own case a friend in her school took her to a terrible godfather and she was told that only two thing they can do to assist her; is either they make the other girl run mad or they killed the girl, on hearing these, my friend just used the excuse of going to buy some items they asked her to buy for this wicked acts and she never returned there. It was the driver that was taking the mother and daughter to the evil herbalist exposed this second friend owned enemies to the elder of the church.

My question is this, why all these blasphemies in the body of Christ? If all will be sincere and pray to God, He creates us, He alone knows what is good for the individual. Jeremiah 29:11, 30:18, 2 Chronicle

7:14, John 6:37b, 17:6, 9, 10:28. But I want to quickly make it clear here; that it is not that necessarily safe to marry someone because he or she is a member of your church. Some young people consider it a green light to get married if their friend is a member of their church and comes from a respectable church-going families, so far, this is fine and is as it ought to be; but a severe test should be applied, as per, has God led you to him or her and is he or she destine to complement you on your living purpose on Earth? Genesis 2:18. Because it is very clear that some church members are carnal and not born again Christians. You need much prayer and put your friend to the test of the Word of God if he or she has a mark of Christian values and Vitality in his or her life. On the other hand remember that God created us one male and one female; therefore, there is only one person or spouse for individual at particular time – And again you may ask; if he or she would be your real missing rib of which God help you to found, as per making you into completeness and wholeness Genesis 2:20:22, Proverb 18:22, 19:14? At this point, I remember the Story of a blessed memory our beloved Apostle Ayo Joseph Babalola one of the Papa in Faith and Pioneered of Christ Apostolic Church and John Wesley these two great servants of God learned their lesson in a very hard way. Though they succeeded largely in ministry, yet it was a tough war on them from the home front and the legacy they left behind on the home front was not too good. Your marriage is a limit when it causes you to sigh, regret, and weep, with wayward spouse and ungodly children. One of the true reasons for marriage according to word of God is to produce Godly offspring Malachi 2:15

I was told that God told Apostle Babalola to marry a deceased man of God's widow, but he rather obey the voice of man with the suggestion of Leviticus 21:13-15 above God command in Ezekiel 44:22 by marrying a single lady in the church environ; those of us familiar with the story know what happen and how Baba ministry that could have lasted for many more years was cut short when he died at age of 55th and from what I heard, immediately Baba died I was told that mama became born again. This is not a funny experience; please pray through to God to the point of obedience so that you will not pray unseemly prayer later. And remember this; as you lay you bed, so you lie on it.

From 1 Thessalonians 4:6-7, it is clear that competition between two people for one partner is hated by God. This is something we should consider carefully, that no man (Anthropos) goes beyond and defrauds his brother in these matters. What matters? It is either in Relationship, Career, Finances, and Positions or any other aspect of life. Many romance stories involve two men competing for the love of one woman or vice versa. This should not be so with those who seek to be guided by the Lord in these matters.

In other words, this mostly and specifically to sisters, please do not fight for a man that has not ask for your hand in marriage and even if he does and you discovered that he is developing a cold feet and or seeing him with another woman, do not raise dust or start throwing stone rather just go on your knees and pray about this and God Almighty our Creator who sees, hear and can able to do that which would only be the best to our interest, desires and values will give divine directions and that which is His perfect will – see the testimonies I gave on this above on this chapter

In Proverbs 30 Agur talks about three things that are too wonderful for him; one of these is "the way of a man with a maid"! The romance of choosing a partner and the way this happens to us as guided by God is something very special for the different individuals involved. Our Lord spent all night in prayer before He chose His disciples, and to be guided by the will of God we need to be similarly exercised in prayer. You need to obey this Word of God in the Leviticus in other to enjoy Genesis 1:28.

There is a different role for the man and the woman in these things. The man has the responsibility to take the initiative, the woman has the responsibility to respond, or not, as the Lord may lead. The man, therefore, has the duty to wait patiently upon the Lord before intervening in the life of a sister, and the woman to prayerfully wait upon the Lord to provide her with His choice.

Marriage is for the raising of godly children in a secure loving environment. We see the problem in society where children are raised without this security, and the instability it brings to children when this is broken

"A man" would indicate a mature person who is able to take the positive decision to "leave" his parents, and the responsibility that goes with that decision. "Cleave" would indicate a bond of affection, which is enduring; literally to glue or cement, a permanent relationship of love. Being "one flesh" would indicate oneness of activity and purpose and also the physical relationship.

Marriage is the God-given relationship for the display of our natural affections and desires. Marriage is until the Lord shall come or death breaks the bond. Matthew 19:6 says "What God hath joined together let not man put asunder."

In marriage too, an individual loses his own identity and both become a new person: "And they twain shall be one flesh: so that they are no more twain but one flesh." Matthew 10:8 If we take Christ as our pattern we should give our love to our partner, wanting only their love in return. (He loved us and gave Himself for us. Ephesians 5:25) and as this is displayed love will grow.

The husband has the role of responsibility as head and the wife the subject position. This is God's order to which we must be prepared to submit if we wish His blessing Ephesians 5:22 and 23 "Wives submit yourselves unto your own husband, as unto the Lord. For the husband is the head of the wife."

If you are considering marriage are you prepared to share everything with your partner as one person: yourself, your time, your money, your interests, your friends so that all you do will be only that which you are both happily agreed upon before the Lord Ephesians 5:21 says "Submitting yourselves one to another in the fear of the Lord." The Lord has decreed that marriage is for life and if we want the Lord's blessing we must follow his instructions. It is the lie of the devil that we can be happy with someone else. We must reject his subtle whispers.

The more we get to know and trust our Father, we will experience that He gives only good gifts to His children. He knows whether or not we are best to be married, and He knows how we will be able to serve Him best Matthew 7:9, Luke 11:11, so if we are to remain single we know that His will is best - indeed in 1 Corinthians chapter 7 Paul says that to remain single is better. If He wants us to be married He will have prepared a partner for us before we were born and He knows best how to bring us together. Only as led in the will of God will these things be enjoyed to the full if we leave the choice of our partner to God: His choice and in His time. Pray to God to show you His way, don't decide what you want and then pray about it. Pray that He may make His mind clear to you and then you will be able to thank Him when He gives the aspect to consider and that is our responsibility to act according to the Scriptures and with wisdom. Prayer for wisdom and direction is as essential in this area as it is in every aspect of our lives. There have been many that have made mistakes: remember Samson and Delilah; Esau and the daughters of Heth; Solomon and his many wives; Ahab and Jezebel.

The Scripture is clear that it is quite wrong for a Christian to marry an unbeliever: The Scripture does not say much about engagement but it does refer to several places to betrothal or espousal. This is shown in the case of Mary and Joseph and mentioned in the Song of Solomon. Engagement is a time when a man and woman are preparing for a marriage to which they have committed themselves. As we have already seen Scripture clearly speaks about the relationship between one man and one woman. Engagement should, therefore, be seen as a serious step of firm commitment to marry (having received clear guidance from the Lord in the decision) and not as a trial period. I would hasten to say that should a mistake be realised before one is married it would be far better to admit it and end the relationship than to continue in a path which is not the Lord's will.

Engagement is a time to prepare yourselves for a new life and attend to the many practical matters that need to be sorted out: a wedding to prepare; a new home to find, and studies to complete for example. First and foremost, however, the engagement period should be used to grow closer together spiritually, mentally and physically (with self-control). The length of an engagement will vary according to different circumstances. If there is a clear knowledge of the Lord's will, there is no reason to delay, it could be frustrating to wait too long before the full enjoyment of living and working together can be enjoyed; especially if the couple are in the same town and see each other often. This, of course, is only my personal view.

Engagement should be used to get to know each other by talking over different matters; praying together and reading God's word. Habits formed at this stage will provide a foundation for married life. In discussing all the many practical aspects of our lives in an attitude of dependence on our Lord and commitment to Him, He will guide our thoughts together and set our aim to serve Him. It is natural to want to spend as much time as possible in each other's company, but let us ensure that we make time for our responsibility to serve the Lord together in our local assembly or wherever He leads. These are all foundations for a spiritual marriage. If we use this time well it will be something to remember with pleasure.

The whole of Scripture is full of the errors of fornication (Acts 15:29) and adultery (Exodus 20:14). The first is sexual relationship outside of marriage and the second sexual relationship with a married person. We must clearly state that physical affection is only intended by God for one man and one woman and that within the confines of marriage. Flee youthful lusts." 2 Timothy 2:22. Choosing to live together rather than marry is prevalent in the world around us. This is clearly fornication; there is no commitment to marry and no public declaration of marriage. The laws of most countries state that marriage must be lawfully enacted and Romans 13:1 tells us "The powers that be; are ordained of God", they must, therefore, be obeyed.

You deserve to be with someone who truly loves you and interested in making your relationship thrives. If you are mistreated or disrespected in any way, think twice before moving forward. Take very seriously problems such as addiction, large debt, uncontrollable emotions, or severe mental illness. You can have tremendous compassion for people with these issues, but the likelihood of being in a satisfying relationship with them is negligible.

Dear friends never married because of Beauty, Statures or age, Fames and Money, Culture and Tribes or under undue influence and duress. In other words you can marry any Tribes as a child of God provided God is the one that brought you two together; though an adage say there was no way a cloud will be white without a stripes of black; - that is to say; a divine and perfect will of God may have some stripes of up and down but it is far better and blessing when God knows, involves and He is the foundations 1 Peter 3:17, 4:19, Hebrew 11:12. And also just because you fall into a mistake and a man dis-virgin you and this make you blindly stick to him for marriage is foolishness and wrong, no matter your conditions of sin, Christ has redeemed us all from the curse of Law Galatians 3:13.

Do not be like one of my aunt and a Pastor daughter who was deflowered by another younger pastor in 1980s, went ahead into Holy Matrimony with him under undue influences; for many years there was no children and the family of the young pastor force him to marry another young girl that gave birth to children and this, my aunt, was sent packing, as at three years ago, I did not hear good news of change about her, the only thing I heard was that the pastor died and the young girl that allowed herself to become the second wife become young widow. Did you see now that you do not need to force yourself on anybody, especially when your creator is not signing your agreement with the person? God, our creator is a merciful Father to forgive and even forget when we sincerely fall into Sin 2 Corinthians 5:21, Psalm 86:5, 130:4, Isaiah 55:7, Jeremiah 33:8.

Whenever, finding a marriage partner? 'GOD'S WAY' is the way of true blessing and Eternal and You can only marry by the clear leading of the Lord and who He choose for you. Your marriage has a major role to play in your life and destiny or ministry, and Marriage should be enjoyed, it should be bliss, not hiss. Your marriage should add to and multiply your life in totality, not subtract from you. Your marriage will lift you to higher level of grace, power, success and maturity if you build it on the leading of your Creator

PERSONAL EXPERIENCE

I remember in 1998 on a Weekend day of Saturday, I just felt to bring out the lists of my loved ones and start praying for them, I got to the set of them that are believing God for Children and I heard Very clearly and audible voice) He said with a Sharp expression 'They are not in my Will' I open my eyes and got up, the environment I stayed then was always quiet, I step out I did not see anyone, it was then I agreed that God might have spoken. I was startled but what I could not place properly was either God meant all the names comprise in this situations or the particular one I just mention before He spoke.

Dear friends, Marriage in the will of God are uplifted; your marriage is meant to be a lift to your God's purpose of life and work, not limits.

DIVORCE

Marriage was the first institution established by God in the book of Genesis, chapter 2. It is a holy covenant that symbolizes the relationship between Christ and his Bride, or the Body of Christ.

The most Bible believer and Christian faith teach that divorce is to be seen only as a last resort after every possible effort toward reconciliation has failed 'No' is wrong. Just as Bible teaches us to enter into marriage carefully and reverently, divorce is to be avoided at all costs. Honouring and upholding the marriage vow brings honour and glory to God.

In Biblical Christian marriage and Union, the bride and groom promise to be faithful to each other "until death do us part." This is also the state for civil marriages; they last until either a divorce or death terminates the relationship.

In earlier generations, this question was very seldom raised, simply because divorce was almost never encountered among Christians and was unusual even in the general population. Today, however, it has become a very real problem in evangelical and Gospel Christian circles. Infidelity is no longer rare, even among Christian leaders, and one can hear almost weekly of some new pastoral "affair" and this has a traumatic effect on His church. With such examples in the leadership, it is bound to be even more common among the ordinary members, and the resulting decline in the stability of the Christian home today is surely one of the more alarming signs of the times.

In today generation you see a man and woman living together before declaring their intentions of love to God and man, with the excuse that they want to know each order properly. My question is this; how many of this pattern have worked out the way they seem; at the end of playing game on each other's; one will come afterward and say my pastor say this or their parent say that; they see revelation, they prophesy that they should not marry a fair girl or a short man, different kinds of lies just to end the relationships, some of this relationship were for many years ranging from 1-10 years of which each of one of them have contributed to each other in terms of blood, energy, money, emotions and time.. This seems to me; 'Very Wrong'. Compare to the biblical view on marriage and a marriage foundation God Almighty laid down that which was confirmed in the book of Genesis and or our older patterns of Marriage whereby the father of the man or woman will take journey on research to get the best partners for their children; to the extent of asking the kind of general sickness of each family or if they have history of madness or terrible history that cannot be told and or if the couple in question are compactable or not they would even make a research if there is going to be long life, enough riches to carry on the family and if there will be children all these in their own way and believe they make enquiries; of which many marriages of today do not care about and that is the reason for massive rate of Divorce in our World and even in the church. Men are not in the place of prayers to seek the mind of Divine True God and sister are not even ready to hear confirmation of their proposal from God; all is that if the man is working in a big company or if he has a big car is all they are after. Naturally, our human natures do not want to suffer but consider those true testimonies I shared in chapters above in this book.

First of all, the divine standard for marriage is a lifelong commitment to one's spouse, and nothing else. Even though divorce was permitted in some cases under the Old Testament economy, Christ made it plain that this was not God's ideal. When He was asked this very question,

"He answered and said unto them, have ye not read, that He which Made them at the beginning made them Male and Female, and said, for this cause shall a man leave father and mother, and shall cleave to his wife; and they shall be one flesh? Wherefore they are no more twain, but one flesh. What therefore God hath joined together, let not man put asunder" Mathew 19:4-6.

There was an adage that says 'where two elephants fought, the grass will not grow again', to some extent it was true, the subject that suffered the effect of divorce is not the only couples but mostly their children, church, and society. Do you know that the church is the cause of the evil that lurked and even stayed in her midst? In the early church setting the Apostle and Disciples did not allow wickedness and evil to snatch away anyone of them, they gather together and always pray for the deliverance of others among them, take for example when enemies got hold of John baptize bible did not give us record that someone or his followers pray on his behalf; may be the daughters of jezebel would not have succeeded in removing his head from his neck Meanwhile, the same incident happen to Peter and the bible record that the church earnestly prays for him and God sent His angel to deliver Peter from the hand of enemies and their prison.

In the same manner I still believe that the church, the God's family; can earnestly pray for the will of God in marriage for their Youth no matter the background they may come from; the power of God superseded any earthly Family uproars; we can pray for the will of God to stay and abide in our midst and if we see any of our beloved one's going through some shaking in marriage it is the church responsibility to save that marriage from falling apart by earnestly contending for the truth of God to stay in Marriage Genesis 3:16, Malachi 2:14-16.

The issue of divorce has a great negative effect mostly on children that are young and who are not even under the good family setting and or a member of the True gospel church who can take up good responsibilities of them. And moreover, any divorce the church allow will definitely cause extra and unnecessary miles of responsibility on their behalf, and if by negligence a Family and church cannot handle this kind of children, they in return turn to an unbearable thorn to society and I am sure most of the time, the effects of this delinquency cannot be easily tackled with. When your Marriage is going through some up and down think very well check within yourself, look before you leap and even leaping is not the next and best solutions, you need to know is there any traits or characters causing nagging and problem between the two all the time of which you need to let go or compromise for the sake of your spouse? I think some few days of separation is allowed and it should be the period of critical of oneself examination and prayers of which the couple should quickly come together and settle for heaven sake 1 Corinthians 7:5

In the book Ephesians 4:31, 32 "Let all bitterness, and wrath, and anger, and clamour, and evil speaking, be put away from you, with all malice: And be ye kind one to another, tender-hearted, forgiving one another, even as God for Christ's sake hath forgiven you."

The first thing people do when they want a divorce is looked for excuses to justify it. Sadly, the easiest place to find excuses today is in your local church. This is tragic! Something is very wrong! You'd think that the one place divorce would be discouraged is in a New Testament Church. Unfortunately, there's a group of ignorant believers today who teach that it's good to get a divorce if one's spouse commits adultery. This is NOT Biblical.

In marriage to be a man is to be godly, committed and responsible, real marriage has to go beyond romance, sex, beauty, pity and materialism into divine reality or purpose and responsibilities.

I heard one of the papas in faith says something some years back, he said since the day God made him understand that he married who he is; since that day he stops finding fault in mama. Therefore, either we believe this or we forget it; we marries who we are, either in perfect will of God or in His permissive will, either the spouse we allow God to bring into our life or the one we take out of lust, infatuations, disobedience and or ignorance Psalms 18:25-26 and 30.

Millions of so-called "Christian" wives and husband have divorced their spouses for insignificance sins. Nearly every pastor, Bible teacher and Christian counsellor today foolishly teaches that divorce is permissible in the case of adultery. This is not so - Where do they put the grace of forgiveness? And on the other hand; for the fact that you have a good Christian spouse does not license you to misbehave and think you will always have your way "NO" - If your spouse cannot deal with you remember we all have a great God tender in mercy and the same times a Judge and more also; He is a consuming Fire. Thessalonians 1:5-6, Act 10:34-35.

The Pharisees came to Jesus, asking Him if it was right to divorce for every cause … "The Pharisees also came unto him, tempting him, and saying unto him, Is it lawful for a man to put away his wife for every cause?" (Matthew 19:3). Jesus answered them by reiterating the permanence of the marriage bond … "Wherefore they are no more twain, but one flesh. What therefore God hath joined together, let not man put asunder" (Matthew 19:6).

The Pharisees didn't hear what they wanted to hear. If (as so many apostate ministers teach today) divorce were permissible in cases of adultery, then Jesus certainly would have responded very differently to the Pharisees question; BUT, He didn't. Jesus reinforced the importance of keeping one's marriage vows. So the Pharisees pushed the issue, demanding an answer from the Lord about divorce … "They say unto him, why did Moses then command to give a writing of divorcement, and to put her away?" (Matthew 19:7). The Pharisees, as do many heathens today, were looking for justification for the sin of divorce - Jesus would not give it to them.

The Pharisees came to Jesus with the same question that many people ask today, i.e., "Is it right to divorce if one's spouse commits adultery?" Here is what Jesus told them in Matthew 19:8 ... "Moses because of the hardness of your hearts suffered you to put away your wives: but from the beginning, it was not so." This was Jesus' response to the question about divorce in the case of adultery. Jesus did not say divorce was permissible. The Pharisees had asked Jesus twice about the possibility of a divorce, and Jesus refuted their reasoning both times. This clearly and irrefutably evidences that the Lord Jesus Christ does not approve of divorce. It is only because of a wicked, stubborn, HARD heart that a person refuses to forgive and be reconciled with their repentant spouse.

Some people try to justify divorce by quoting Matthew 5:32 and Matthew 19:9; but any honest Bible student knows that proper Bible exegesis of any particular Scripture requires a comparison with all other related Scriptures. Matthew 5:32 properly explains Matthew 19:9. Matthew 5:32 states, "But I say unto you, that whosoever shall put away his wife, saving for the cause of fornication, causes her to commit adultery: and whosoever shall marry her that is divorced committed adultery." Jesus was actually condemning divorce in this Scripture. In other words, "Any man who divorces his wife is causing her to commit adultery in remarriage unless she was already guilty of adultery, in which case the man would not be blamed for causing her to commit adultery." However, this Scripture in no way diminishes the sin of divorce. There is NOTHING in Matthew 5:32 that permit divorce. Matthew 19:9 has the same meaning.

The word except fornication and indecency in Matthew 19:9 in the other version of the bible may have difficult translation for many, there may be a misrepresentation of this from the original context of this biblical verse; whichever application, this could be an indecency in case of INCEST Deuteronomy 22:30, 27:20, 1 Corinthians 5:1 and or Idolatry 1 Corinthians 7:15.

The key Scripture when speaking of divorce is Matthew 19:8 ... "Moses because of the hardness of your hearts suffered you to put away your wives: but from the beginning, it was not so." Matthew 19:8, when compared with other Scriptures on divorce, quickly shoots down all the modern apostates who teach that Jesus allowed divorce. No Sir! That is not what the Bible teaches. Jesus plainly stated that divorce is always the result of a sinful HARD-HEART.

REMARRIAGE FORBIDDEN FOR THAT WHO DIVORCE

In Mark 10:11-12, Jesus plainly stated ... "Whosoever shall put away his wife, and marry another, committed adultery against her. And if a woman shall put away her husband, and be married to another, she committed adultery." I heard a well-known Bible scholar say that the Bible only prohibits divorce, but remarriage of divorced people is right. He's dead wrong! Mark 10:11 proves him a liar. If a woman divorces her husband, she is absolutely forbidden from getting remarried. To remarry is adultery! 1 Corinthians 7:10-11, "And unto the married I command, yet not I, but the Lord, Let not the wife depart from her husband: But and if she departs, let her remain unmarried, or be reconciled to her husband: and let not the husband put away his wife." Very few preachers are involved in the ministry of reconciliation of marriages, but this is what the Bible teaches. A divorced woman, if she filed, has no right to remarry, and is Biblically forbidden to do so. God will judge all offenders 2 Corinthians 5:10

DID GOSPELS AGREED ON THESE ISSUES? YES.

Mark 10:12 warns, "And if a woman shall put away her husband, and be married to another, she committed adultery." And again in Luke 16:18 we read, "Whosoever put away his wife, and marries another, committed adultery: and whosoever marries her that is put away from her husband committed adultery." Matthew is the only Apostle writer who seems to give an exception to the rule, i.e., permission to divorce.

It is abundantly clear to me, and I think also to any honest Bible student, that Matthew's account must be interpreted in view of those of Mark and Luke as well. There can be no conflict between the Gospels. Neither Mark nor Luke spoke of any justification for divorce. Thus, I believe it is wrong to conclude that Jesus allowed for divorce in Matthew; when Mark and Luke clearly do not agree with such speculation.

Too many people interpret the Bible by always looking for the exception to the rule. Thus, should it be surprising that Godless feminists have developed their own Feminist Theology? Should it be surprising that homosexuals have rewritten their own Bible, Satanists, fornicators, sodomites, and atheists will quote the Bible in an attempt to prove their point? And yes, so do many heathens manipulate the Scriptures in an attempt to whitewash their sin of divorce.

For Example in 1 Corinthian 7:15, "but if the unbeliever leaves, let it be so. The brother or the sister is not bound in such circumstances; God has called us to live in peace" Those who remarry without Biblical authority are living in continuous adultery because they are still bound to their first spouse as long as that spouse lives 1 Corinthians 7:39

The teaching here is the Christian is not under the bondage of having to give up his salvation and forsake Christ to please his spouse. A Christian must not abandon Christ simply to hold on to his unbelieving mate. The loyalty of the Christian belongs first to Christ. To such bondage Christians do not have to submit to in order to hold on to their marriage. Marriage is not a slave/

master relationship. Divorce and remarriage are not under discussion anywhere in 1 Corinthians 7. In all 40 verses of this chapter the only authority for remarriage is given in verses 9 & 39 and that is only in case of the death of a spouse.

THE HYPOCRISY OF DIVORCE

Jesus' disciples asked Him how many times they were required to forgive a fallen brother. In Matthew 18:22 Jesus responded ... "I say not unto thee, until seven times: but, until seventy times seven." How is it then that the same pastor who believes that Jesus taught to forgive 490 TIMES, doesn't believe in forgiving even once in the case of a spouse guilty of adultery? Hypocrites! Jesus taught unlimited forgiveness; BUT divorce offers no mercy, no forgiveness, no reconciliation, and no hope of a happily reunited marriage. Oh, how God hates the sin of divorce! Malachi 2:16 Divorce is a sin of self-righteousness, where a person declares them self; less sinful and; therefore, possessing the right to abandon, forsake and divorce their spouse. James 2:10 shows just how wicked we all are ... "For whosoever shall keep the whole law, and yet offend in one point, he is guilty of all." You're just as sinful, selfish, as you think your spouse is.

GOD HATES DIVORCE!

You know, why is it that many people who want a divorce go around quoting Jesus' statement on adultery; but I never hear these people quote Malachi 2:16 where God say he HATES divorce, "For the LORD, the God of Israel, saith that he hateth putting away." "Putting away" is the Old Testament term used for divorce, which is an interesting phrase. The term "putting away" comes from the Hebrew word shalach, and literally means "to forsake, to cast or push away." When you divorce your spouse, you are literally shoving them away from you, forsaking them, and God HATES IT.

There is NO bigger lie today than that divorce is permissible in cases of adultery. There are NO Biblical grounds for divorce. It's perplexing to me that a professed Gospel "minister" would recommend someone gets a divorce, in lieu of a Bible that teaches forgiveness from cover to cover. Is divorce forgiveness? What about the sins of murder, theft, and assault? You can't show me grounds for divorce for these sins. Matthew 5:28 teaches that ALL MEN are adulterers!

Therefore, dear friend you need to be born of God and His divine spirit, pray for His divine Will in marriage and you will not marry a man or a rib that is not your own.

When a man takes a wife and marries her, if then she finds no favour in his eyes because he has found some indecency in her, and he writes her a certificate of divorce and puts it in her hand and sends her out of his house, and she departs out of his house, and if she goes and becomes another man's wife, and the latter man hates her and writes her a certificate of divorce and puts it in her hand and sends her out of his house, or if the latter man dies, who took her to be his wife, then her former husband, who sent her away, may not take her again to be his wife, after she has been defiled, for that is an abomination before the LORD. And you shall not bring sin upon the land that the LORD your God is giving you for an inheritance Deuteronomy 24:1-4.

And this second thing you do. You cover the LORD's altar with tears, with weeping and groaning because he no longer regards the offering or accepts it with favour from your hand. But you say, "Why does he not?" Because the LORD was a witness between you and the wife of your youth, to whom you have been faithless, though she is your companion and your wife by covenant. Did he not make them one, with a portion of the Spirit in their union? AND WHAT WAS GOD SEEKING IN MARRIAGE IF NOT GODLY OFFSPRING?

So guard yourselves in your spirit, and let none of you be faithless to the wife of your youth. "For the man who does not love his wife but divorces her, says the LORD, the God of Israel, covers his garment with violence, says the LORD of hosts. So guard yourselves in your spirit, and do not be faithless." Malachi 2:13-16.

"It was also said, 'Whoever divorces his wife, let him give her a certificate of divorce.' But I say to you that everyone who divorces his wife, except or paraphrases "because" on the ground of sexual immorality, makes her commit adultery, and whoever marries a divorced woman commits adultery Matthew 5:31-32.

For a married woman is bound by law to her husband while he lives, but if her husband dies she is released from the law of marriage. Accordingly, she will be called an adulterous if she lives with another man while her husband is alive. But if her husband dies, she is free from that law, and if she marries another man she is not an adulterous Roman 7:2-3

To the married I give this charge (not I, but the Lord): the wife should not separate from her husband (but if she does, she should remain unmarried or else be reconciled to her husband), and the husband should not divorce his wife.

To the rest, I say (I, not the Lord) that if any brother has a wife who is an unbeliever, and she consents to live with him, he should not divorce her. If any woman has a husband who is an unbeliever, and he consents to live with her, she should not divorce him for the unbelieving husband is made holy because of his wife and the unbelieving wife is made holy because of her husband. Otherwise, your children would be unclean, but as it is, they are holy. But if the unbelieving partner separates, let it be so. In such cases, the brother or sister is not enslaved. God has called you to peace 1 Corinthians 7:10-15.

A wife is bound to her husband as long as he lives. But if her husband dies, she is free to be married to whom she wishes, only in the Lord 1 Corinthians 7:39.

"One flesh" You can't get more joined than that; it has to be 1+1=1. Also, marriage is a covenant, a vow, a promise, an oath. God is very serious about such a thing.

If a man vows a vow unto the LORD or swears an oath to bind his soul with a bond; he shall not break his word, he shall do according to all that proceeded out of his mouth. If a woman also vows a vow unto the LORD, and bind herself by a bond, being in her father's house in her youth; And her father hears her vow, and her bond wherewith she hath bound her soul, and her father shall hold his peace at her: then all her vows shall stand, and every bond wherewith she hath bound her soul shall stand. Numbers 30:2

When thou shall vow a vow unto the LORD thy God, thou shalt not slack to pay it: for the LORD thy God will surely require it of thee, and it would be sin in thee. Deuteronomy 23:21

But all the princes said unto the entire congregation, we have sworn unto them by the LORD God of Israel: now, therefore, we may not touch them. 20 This we will do to them; we will even let them live, lest wrath is upon us, because of the oath which we swore unto them. Joshua 9:19

And let none of you imagine evil in your hearts against his neighbour; and love no false oath: for all these are things that I hate, saith LORD Zechariah 8:17

That's just a few of the verses but it is clear. God takes vow seriously and expects it to be kept. If not there will be consequences. It does not take much reading of the bible to see that covenant breaking has led to flaming death and destruction. It is clear that many have come to see breaking a covenant as changing the mind. It is much more than that. It is betrayal, turning the vow into a lie.

The law and the prophets were until John: since that time the kingdom of God is preached, and every man pressed into it. And it is easier for heaven and earth to pass, than one little of the law to fail. Whosoever put away his wife and marries another, committed adultery: and whosoever marries her that is put away from her husband committed adultery Luke 16:16-18.

So in truth there is only one way God truly allows marriage to end; In Romans 7:1-3 - Know ye not, brethren, (for I speak to them that know the law,) how that the law hath dominion over a man as long as he lives? For the woman which hath a husband is bound by the law to her husband so long as he lives; but if the husband is dead, she is loosed from the law of her husband. So then if, while her husband lives, she be married to another man, she shall be called an adulterous: but if her husband is dead, she is free from that law; so that she is no adulteress, though she is married to another man. Therefore that is why we say till death do us part.

May God bless you all and may He bless your marriage even, as we strive to obey His truth till eternity Rev 20:12, 21:7-8

HEALTH

The traditions, ignorance, and manmade doctrine had made us believe that sickness and illness are the will of God in other to glorify His divine name; 'No' it is a wrong believe. Throughout the scripture, we can see that sickness and ailments are a curse Deuteronomy 28:20-28, 58-61.

It is a divine principle and pattern of divine Godhead for His children to always be in perfect health even as we are living in this terrible world of flesh and sin. God providentially and always provides a way of escape from our dilemma and calamity we found ourselves as a result of sin and or ignorance that is why when Christ was on earth He always heal all manners of diseases and deliverance from demons. To be in perfect health is children bread because Godhead made and or created Herbs for our meat Genesis 1:29, Number 11:7:9, Matthew 15:26, Hebrew 6:7, 1Kings 21:2.

In biblical era Herbs are not only for food but were also for flavor and for medicinal purposes. It was used by the Egyptians and Hebrews for incense, cosmetics, perfumes, and medicines. It was also used at that time for embalming. It was considered, for example; as it were for Frankincense and Myrrh, these are a rare treasure and were so thought to be a great gift for Christ when He was a baby. Frankincense has a gummy resin derived from the shrub: Nowadays, it is used in treating sore throats, infected gums, thrush, calming, soothing and athlete's foot and also contains cleansing agents.

In the book of 1 Corinthians 3:16 ("Don't you know that you are God's temple and that God's Spirit lives in you?") – This practical text is based on sound, cutting-edge People who lived in Jesus' time were wonderful herbalists (They were Herbs analyst and professional practitioners; (not herbalist Wizard or evil magic juju practitioner). Scientific research and Christian principles as such, it provides an exciting new approach to teaching health and wholeness to help meet part of the Christian benefits and make community disease free Jeremiah 29:11.

The Wholeness of our being is focused on how we are made, how we are made to move, how we are to be nourished, and how we are to behave on our path to Wholeness.

In God's purpose and biblical reasons we are to value our wholeness, fitness, and Health, these are parts of our own life's mission; to explore our body image, eating disorders, nutritional and emotional health and wholeness. The issues of our Health comprise also; the wholeness and right way as it relates to our sleep habits and personal relationships.

The sketch about health in this book encourages the true Christian to develop a comprehensive strategy to maintain personal wholeness in a relationship with God and His divine principles as it were laid down in the scriptures I believe it will go a long way, couple with holiness and obedient to rules of life. 3 John 1:2. Psalm 136:25, I advise that you read carefully the nutritional value in each product you are buying and see if they contain these lists below for your nutritional values and benefits Genesis 6:21

In God's purpose and biblical reasons we are to value our wholeness, fitness, and Health, these are parts of our own life's mission; to explore our body image, eating disorders, nutritional and emotional health and wholeness.

The issues of our Health comprise also; the wholeness and right way as it relates to our sleep habits and personal relationships. I heard some people say even in their preaching that as a Christian you should not sleep more than three to four hours a day – please, careful of whom you listening to because, good advice may not be godly counsel Even the bible gave us many instant passages of having quality Rest

Basil leaves: - (Efinrin – Scent leaf) could help strengthen the body's immune system, an Antioxidant natural cure for the respiratory system, stomach pain, stomach worms as well as cramps.

Bitter leaves: the juice could help in regulating diabetes, itching, constipation, worm, fever/malaria and weight-loss.

Wild Gourd (Eso Bara) this could be of help in treating fibroid and pile; once a while in minimal proportion clean out the seeds and blend with very ripe pawpaw, it's good for cleaning internal bowel. It is not good for pregnant woman.

Some foods are free for daily and or are for often consumptions, in another hand you can take them anytime you like, such as- Water, Green tea with skimmed milk without sugar, fruits as; Pawpaw, Mangoes, Watermelon, Oranges and Raw Vegetable as per; garden egg, Cucumber, Carrot, Cabbage and Tomatoes

All these Plants, fruits and Herbs listed above are scientifically proven by Christian Doctors and they were all provided by God Almighty for our meat and they are all available for use, for our wholeness and healthy living Genesis 1:29. Genesis 9:3, Psalm 104:14.

There are three strong antioxidants, and they are; the beta–carotene and vitamins-C and E. Each of these nutrients have been shown to be very effective against age-related illnesses such as cancer and heart disease. Although you can get some protection by taking antioxidant supplements, most doctors agree that the antioxidants in super foods are a better choice and should be your first line of defence. It's best to get them through foods like fruits and vegetables, where they exist in the proportions nature intended.

I suggest you eat more of bitter-leaf and basil leaves in your soup more often also I remembered that my GP refer me to Nutritionist and I was told to go for fruits and fruits such as Banana, Cabbage and Watermelon prevent heart attack while plum apple and Carrot are anti-cancer

The quickest way to get vitamin-C, for example, is to have a glass of grapefruit juice, an orange, pepper spices such as in Pepper soup, each of which provides more than 100 percent of the Daily Recommended Allowance (DRA). For beta-carotene, deep green or bright orange fruits and vegetables are your best picks in your battle against aging. Nuts and seeds are also good sources of vitamin-E.

Dear friends, above all, Holiness and Godliness are a great gain to longevity. Cleanliness, Regular check-up with your doctor if you have one, quality Rest; and good quality of sleep (not laziness kinds- Proverbs 20:13) with some kinds of physical exercises in our day to day activities can go a long way for our good benefits and wholeness Ecclesiastics 5:12, Proverbs 3:24.

I Suggest that Holiness, Godliness, and Contentment are Far Better and Safer For Healthy Living 1Timothy 4:8, 6:6, Proverbs 15:16, 22:4, Hebrews 12:14. The Spirit of God is still in the business of healing especially when you have tried all you could, and prove abortive turn to Him He heals instantly, the Spirit of divine God remains great and the same forever. James 5:14, Exodus 23:25. In another word; worship the true Godhead, follow His divine Principle and Pattern, think no evil, do no evil, have clean hands and a pure heart, be yourself, do not over anxious and do not compare yourself with anyone Philippians 4:8. Psalm 15, Psalm 34:14.

PERSONAL TESTIMONY

In 1993, I remembered one of my beloved sisters; a wife to my Evangelist friend who could not eat and drink for two weeks, I do not even know that that was the place his abode, I just went to that house to visit one of the brethren, and I just heard someone call my name and to my surprise it was my Evangelist friend, I asked after his wife and he told me she was inside very sick sitting in one place, that she could not move, eat or drink, Ah.. I was surprised, and I went inside lay a hand on her and pray a simple prayer of faith of a young teenage girl, to the faithfulness of God, I am telling you the gospel truth, instantly she was healed and finished a bowl of Pap made for her that very day after the prayer.

GOD BLESS YOU RICHLY

Printed in the United States
By Bookmasters